Praise for *Vincent van Gogh and the Good Samaritan*:

'Reading this book is like experienci~ ~moment in van Gogh's work, when t¹ ~aintings are overwhelmed by the ~t marks his arrival in Provence. I ~illuminated Jesus' parable and Vincent ~.. never see either in the same way again.'

Rt Revd Paul Bayes, Bishop of Liverpool

'Beautifully structured and filled with insights from an author who is both a priest and a painter, Henry's compelling enthusiasm both for Jesus' parable and van Gogh's painting, has produced a book bursting with insights into van Gogh, God and life.'

Revd Professor Maggi Dawn,
Professor of Theology, Durham University

'I have enjoyed this book as much as I can remember ever enjoying any I have read. I am in awe at the breadth of knowledge it displays and the insight and compassion that pulsates through every page. Henry raises myriads of life's important questions and provides suggestions for how to tackle them without once being prescriptive. I learned so much about God, myself, and van Gogh even after decades of musing on all three!'

Rt Revd David Gillett,
formerly Bishop of Bolton and
Principal of Trinity College, Bristol

Vincent van Gogh and the Good Samaritan

The wounded painter's journey

HENRY MARTIN

DARTON · LONGMAN + TODD

First published in Great Britain in 2021 by
Darton, Longman and Todd Ltd
1 Spencer Court
140–142 Wandsworth High Street
London SW18 4JJ

Print book ISBN: 978-1-913657-34-5
eBook ISBN: 978-1-913657-35-2

A catalogue record for this book is available from the British Library.

Interior design by Judy Linard.

Printed and bound in Great Britain by Short Run Press, Exeter

Suicide Awareness

The story of Vincent van Gogh inevitably raises the subjects of self-harm and suicide. We have many more resources available to us today than existed in his time, to support people in crisis. The Zero Suicide Alliance (www.zerosuicidealliance.com) have an excellent free training package. It takes only twenty minutes to complete. One day, when you're not expecting it, it might prove to have been twenty minutes extremely well spent.

In memory of
Trevor Martin 1927 – 2015

Contents

Author's Note

There is more than one system for numbering van Gogh's letters. I have chosen to follow Ronald de Leeuw's lead (as per my Penguin Classics edition of *The Letters of Vincent van Gogh*). I also give, in brackets, the number assigned in the Van Gogh Museum's excellent (and searchable) online collection (vangoghletters.org).

Where I quote directly from van Gogh's letters, the translations are my own, as are the excerpts from Albert Aurier's article of January 1890 in the *Mercure de France*, 'Les Isolés: Vincent Van Gogh'. I am deeply indebted to my friend Charl DeWinter, who patiently went through all my translations of Van Gogh's Dutch with that level of insight possessed only by a native speaker. Quotations from Johanna van Gogh-Bonger's *Memoir of Vincent van Gogh* are taken from her own English translation of her original Dutch version.

All Bible quotations, unless otherwise stated, come from the NRSVA edition.

Vincent van Gogh ... a short biographical time-line

1853   Vincent was born on the 30th of March, in Zundert in the Netherlands.

1869-76 Vincent worked for the art dealers Goupil & Cie, first in The Hague, then London and finally Paris. He also began his lifelong correspondence with his brother, Theo.

1876   From April to December, Vincent lived in England, working in a boarding school in Ramsgate and then as a Methodist minister's assistant in Isleworth.

1878   Having failed to complete his entrance exams for the School of Theology in Amsterdam, Vincent took a three-month course at a protestant missionary school in Laken (near Brussels).

1879   Vincent began work as an evangelist in the Borinage, a coal-mining region in southern Belgium. After six months he was dismissed from his post.

1880   Vincent decided to become an artist.

1881   Vincent fell disastrously in love with his cousin Kee Vos.

1882   Vincent set up a studio in The Hague and started a relationship with Sien Hoornik.

1883   Vincent left Sien to embark on a drawing tour of Drenthe and returned, not to her, but to his parents' house (now in Nuenen).

1885   After the death of his father, Vincent enrolled in an art academy in Antwerp.

1886-88	Vincent moved into his brother Theo's home in Paris.
1888	In February, Vincent moved to Arles in Provence. There he rented the 'Yellow House' and sought to establish a commune of artists. He called his first summer there the 'yellow high note' of his painting career.[1] In October, Paul Gauguin joined him. On the night of the 23rd of December, Vincent cut off his ear with a razor and ended the year in hospital.
1889	On the 8th of May, after a few months of being in and out of hospital, Vincent became a voluntary in-patient at the Saint-Paul-de-Mausole Asylum in Saint-Rémy.
1890	Still in the Asylum, Vincent painted his version of 'The Good Samaritan'. It was finished by the 3rd of May.

On the 16th of May, he left the asylum for Paris and, on the 20th, he arrived in Auvers-sur-Oise as a patient of Dr Paul Gachet. He died on the 29th of July, having shot himself in the chest two days beforehand. |

---

[1] Letter **581** (752), to Theo 24/3/1889.

The Parable of the Good Samaritan

Just then a lawyer stood up to test Jesus. 'Teacher,' he said, 'what must I do to inherit eternal life?' He said to him, 'What is written in the law? What do you read there?' He answered, 'You shall love the Lord your God with all your heart, and with all your soul, and with all your strength, and with all your mind; and your neighbour as yourself.' And he said to him, 'You have given the right answer; do this, and you will live.'

But wanting to justify himself, he asked Jesus, 'And who is my neighbour?'

Jesus replied, 'A man was going down from Jerusalem to Jericho, and fell into the hands of robbers, who stripped him, beat him, and went away, leaving him half dead. Now by chance a priest was going down that road; and when he saw him, he passed by on the other side. So likewise a Levite, when he came to the place and saw him, passed by on the other side. But a Samaritan while travelling came near him; and when he saw him, he was moved with pity. He went to him and bandaged his wounds, having poured oil and wine on them. Then he put him on his own animal, brought him to an inn, and took care of him. The next day he took out two denarii, gave them to the innkeeper, and said, "Take care of him; and when I come back, I will repay you whatever more you spend."

'Which of these three, do you think, was a neighbour to the man who fell into the hands of the robbers?'

He said, 'The one who showed him mercy.' Jesus said to him, 'Go and do likewise.'

Luke 10:26-37

Preface

I have been musing on the enduring popularity of Vincent van Gogh.

It starts with his genius as a painter. Where else could it begin? His vision, his choice of subjects, his outrageous risks with tone and colour, his distinctive brushwork all combine to make his work leap out, even now one hundred and thirty years after his death. And there is so much to see. He was unbelievably prolific. Even after a lifetime of enjoying his work I constantly find pictures that I have never seen before, almost as if he continues to work, somehow sending new paintings through a loop in time, into the museum I am visiting.

Recently, I have been asking friends to list how many nineteenth-century figures can be identified simply from their faces. There are a couple of heads of state, Queen Victoria and Abraham Lincoln. Florence Nightingale gets a mention, but only if she is holding a lamp. Some might recognise Charles Dickens. I do not allow Ghandi or Einstein; technically they were born in the nineteenth century but we only recognise their older twentieth-century faces. The same goes for that gang of brutal dictators, Stalin, Mao, Hitler and so on. We also have this red-bearded Dutchman, sometimes wearing a straw hat and always painted in loose strokes. If anyone had told Vincent van Gogh that his face would become one of the top five most-recognisable of his entire century, surely he would have laughed in disbelief? But the fact remains: his face can appear without introduction in an American comedy (*Modern Family*), on the BBC (*Doctor Who*), or as graffiti on a Taiwanese street, and people know who he is. How did this come about?

It is the art, of course it is the art. Without the art no one would be interested. But there is more to it than just the art. There is also his story, which ticks so many boxes. He is an archetypal underdog; the unrecognised genius, scorned in his own lifetime by a world blind to his talent. There is tragedy; the young man who mutilated his ear and then took his own life. There is irony; the painter who struggled with poverty, whose works now sell for millions.

What strange alchemy might occur when this great nineteenth-century story meets an even greater story, one which dates to the dawn of Christianity and is possibly the most famous of all the parables told by Jesus of Nazareth?

In 2011, I visited the Kröller-Müller Museum in the Netherlands. There I saw an instantly recognisable scene. The Good Samaritan, painted by … well, it can only have been Vincent van Gogh. Who else could paint like that? I asked myself, *'How have I never seen this one before?'*

Over the intervening years I have been wondering, *'Why did he paint this? And why in 1890? Why so near to the end of his life? I thought he was all done with religion by then.'* This book is my attempt to answer these questions, and, if not answer definitively, at least to explore them.

CHAPTER 1

The Question ...'And who is my neighbour?'

'Just then a lawyer stood up to test Jesus. "Teacher," he said, "what must I do to inherit eternal life?" He said to him, "What is written in the law? What do you read there?" He answered, "You shall love the Lord your God with all your heart, and with all your soul, and with all your strength, and with all your mind; and your neighbour as yourself." And he said to him, "You have given the right answer; do this, and you will live." But wanting to justify himself, he asked Jesus, "And who is my neighbour?"'

Luke 10:25-29

Stories do not appear out of thin air. Jesus tells the parable of the Good Samaritan in answer to a question. A lawyer comes to test him, asking what he must do to inherit eternal life. This question is fundamentally flawed, so Jesus responds not with a straight answer but a question of his own. The lawyer quotes an appropriate verse from scripture and the conversation might end here. Only the lawyer still seeks something more, so he adds a supplementary question:

'And who is my neighbour?'

This time Jesus replies not with another question but with the most astonishing story; a story that has gone on to change the world. It has inspired millions of people, from St Augustine to the Reverend Dr Martin Luther King, Jr. It has prompted countless acts of charity. These range from small deeds of everyday goodness to immense world-changing projects. Chad Varah founded 'the Samaritans', the world's first crisis hotline for people at risk of suicide.

Jesus left his parables open. He did not nail down one meaning alone. He allows his listeners to unearth his stories' truths in situ, at whatever point they find themselves in life. He risks being wildly misinterpreted. Margaret Thatcher, for instance, famously quoted this parable, not to promote neighbourly love but to sanctify the amassing of personal wealth. She said, 'No-one would remember the Good Samaritan if he'd only had good intentions; he had money as well.'

Countless others, however, have heard the story and have gone on to perform selfless acts of loving charity, recognising a core truth: that anyone in need is their neighbour.

Like stories, paintings rarely come from nowhere. Vincent van Gogh, as a minister's son, was surely familiar with this parable from an early age. Its influence can be detected throughout his life. However, it was only in 1890, shortly before his death, that he completed this painting. The process began the previous year, with an accident in his room at the Saint-Paul Asylum in Saint-Rémy; a handful of his lithographs fell into some oil and paint and were damaged. One of these was of Eugene Delacroix's 'Pietà'. To overcome his sadness at this loss, he started to paint his own version. He found an unexpected sense of satisfaction in this act of copying.[1] All this is recorded in a letter dated the 10th of September 1889. Vincent left an invaluable record of his thoughts in the form of letters, which means that we can be precise about timings. He wrote mainly to his brother, Theo, but he also corresponded with his parents, his sister and with other artists.

Theo, despite being younger by four years, was Vincent's benefactor. Theo paid his living expenses and provided him with canvases, brushes, papers and paint, and all other such materials

---

[1] Letter **605** (801), to Theo 10/9/1889.

necessary for his vocation. He would send Vincent prints, woodcuts and lithographs of other artists' works. Vincent in turn pinned these onto his walls, surrounding himself with inspiration. His letters tell us that he had a lithograph of Delacroix's 'The Good Samaritan' in his room in Arles, in early May 1889.[2]

I will admit to a sense of disappointment when I learnt that Vincent's Good Samaritan was merely a copy. This is my error arising from my ignorance. I have since learnt that copying was a trusted way for Vincent to learn from those he admired, such as Rembrandt and Millet.[3] On the 19th of September 1889, he wrote to Theo:

'... I want to *learn*. Even if copying is the *old* system, that doesn't worry me at all. I'm going to copy the Good Samaritan by Delacroix too.'

Letter **607** (805), to Theo 19/9/1889

He repeated this intention in the February of 1890.[4] And finally, from the asylum at Saint-Rémy, he noted to Theo on the 3rd of May 1890 that he had completed the work. His actual words were 'J'ai aussi essayé une copie', which translates as 'I have also attempted a copy'.[5] To my ears this sounds rather an understatement. I wish he had been less modest and said more. At least we can date the work with confidence to the spring or early summer of 1890.

He copied the works of several others, even Japanese artists, such as Hiroshige. If nothing else their figures offered a reasonable substitute for the models he perpetually struggled to fund. Once he was in the asylum at Saint-Rémy, models became even harder to find and so he began copying in earnest.[6]

---

[2] Letter **590** (768), to Theo 3/5/1889.
[3] Letter **W14** (804), to Wil 19/9/1889.
[4] Letter **626** (854), to Theo 10 or 11/2/1890.
[5] Letter **632** (866), to Theo 3/5/1890.
[6] Letter **607** (805), to Theo 19/9/1889.

Vincent van Gogh and the Good Samaritan

No doubt today he would exploit the endless vaults of Google Images, but in his day figures, even pictures of figures, were less readily available.

His 'copying' was never slavish; he always painted in his own unique style. He reasoned that he was behaving just like any musician; they are never criticised for performing a piece which they had not composed themselves. In fact, they are expected to bring something of themselves to the work. He wrote to Theo:

> '… whenever someone plays Beethoven, they add their own personal interpretation – with music and even more so with singing – the *interpretation* of a composer is a key factor and there are no hard and fast rules stating that no one but the composer can play their own compositions.
>
> So far so good! Well for me, especially as I am not well at the moment, I'm seeking to do something which will console me for my own pleasure.
>
> I'm taking a black and white version of a Delacroix or a Millet as my models, and then I'm improvising on them using colour; not giving myself complete freedom of course, since I try to remember *their* pictures – and memory gives me a vague recollection of colours which are at least right in feeling, if not completely accurate – that's how I do my interpreting.
>
> Loads of people don't copy, loads of others do – as for myself, I stumbled across it accidentally and I find it teaches me things and above all, at times consoles me.
>
> And then my brush, between my fingers becomes as a bow on a violin and plays absolutely for my pleasure.'
>
> Letter **607** (805), to Theo c. 19/9/1889

If you google Delacroix's 'The Good Samaritan', you will see that the two works are like but not alike. The basic form is the same, albeit inverted; I am guessing that the lithograph was a mirror of the original. Van Gogh's brushstrokes are entirely his own, as is his use of colour, since the lithograph was black and

20

white. We do not know if van Gogh ever saw the original with Delacroix's chosen colours but we can be sure he copied from a print that had strong highlights surrounded by deep shadows. He chose a much more even light and depicts the drama with bright colours, making particular use of yellow.

Vincent van Gogh's religious life

As I read more and more of Vincent's letters, I realised the truly remarkable fact is not that this picture is a copy, but that it is a biblical scene. This took me by surprise as I learnt more of his history with religion, which was turbulent to say the least. Here is a brief summary:

- He was the eldest son of a minister and as such was expected to follow in his father's footsteps. Initially he embraced this notion wholeheartedly.[7]

- At the age of 23 he started to train for the ministry, informally at first, but with the same all-consuming passion that he later gave to his painting.

- His favourite Bible phrase throughout this time was 'sorrowful but always rejoicing'.[8] Hardly buoyant with optimism, it appealed to his melancholy nature. He often entreated Theo to hold close these words, even wearing them as a cloak to protect him from life's storms.[9] If you would like a deeper insight into his mind-set during this period, you can read one of his sermons; he transcribed the full text for Theo's edification.[10]

---

[7] Letter **89** (109), to Theo 22/3/1877 – for more about his father, see Chapter 4 'The Priest'.

[8] 2 Corinthians 6:10.

[9] Letter **89** (109), to Theo 22/3/1877.

[10] enclosed with letter **79** (096) from Isleworth, sermon given by Vincent van Gogh in English on 29th October 1876.

- In 1878, when he was 25, he failed to complete his entrance exams for the School of Theology in Amsterdam.

- In January 1879 he was given a six-month trial as a lay-preacher in the Borinage, a coal mining district in southern Belgium. Local legend remembers 'Monsieur Vincent' as a saint, even an angel: giving his money and clothes away, sleeping on the floor of a hut, carrying coal for pregnant women and caring for the sick.[11] He sought to excise from himself any privileges that stood between him and the local people. The Church's committee took a dim view of this. They were alarmed by his extremism and self-neglect. In the following July, they decided not to renew his contract and he found himself unemployed.

- Vincent became disillusioned. He perceived religious institutions as harsh. He viewed their clergy as full of fine words but distinctly lacking in love. He ran into further confrontations when his desire for love collided with the 'respectable' expectations of church people.

- This disillusionment rapidly grew into an outright rejection of formal Christianity. There were terrible clashes with his father, leading Vincent to adopt the word 'Jesuitisms'. He used this to dismiss any of his father's views that he deemed pious but loveless. It was painful a time all round. Vincent emerged scarred, never to return to the Church. By 1884 he looked back on a time when he was confused by chilling religious ideas. Since losing these, he claimed, his customary warmth had returned.[12]

---

[11] *'In Belgium's Borinage, where Van Gogh the pastor became a painter'* by Mary Winston Nicklin, The Washington Post, 19 February 2015.
[12] Letter **358** (432), to Theo 1/3/1884.

In 1884, he gave the following view of Christ to Theo:

> 'Oh, I am no friend of present-day Christianity, even though its *founder* was sublime – I have seen right through present-day Christianity. That icy coldness mesmerised me in my youth – but since then I have wrought my revenge.'
>
> Letter **378** (464), to Theo, 2/10/1884

By 1887, he had no certainty about a God who might intervene in our human affairs; he wrote to his sister Wil:

> '… I am uncomfortable about accepting for myself or recommending to others, a belief that there are powers above us that personally intervene to help or comfort us. Providence is such a strange thing, and I'll admit to you that I genuinely do not know what to make of it.'
>
> Letter **W1** (574), to Wil, summer or autumn 1887

He went on to develop his own spirituality, based on his respect for love, art, truth and his overwhelming appreciation of nature. We can argue back and forth whether this could be called a religion or not. He never abandoned the notion of God, but insisted that God could not be defined systematically.[13] He saw God more as an artist, whose creation showed clear signs of genius but like an 'overworked sketch' was sloppy and rushed.[14] He remained fascinated by Christ's humanity[15] and regarded his teaching as a set of 'lofty ideals'.[16] Even after abandoning formal

---

[13] Letter **164** (193), to Theo c. 21/12/81, following his comment about the God of the clergy being as dead as a doornail

[14] Letter **490** (613), to Theo van Gogh 26/5/1888.

[15] He was deeply influenced by Renan's *Vie de Jésus*, which argued that argued that Jesus' life should be recorded like any other historical figure and be subjected to the same academic scrutiny. See Letter **587** (763), to Theo van Gogh 28/4/1889.

[16] 'lofty ideals' is van Gogh's own phrase. See Letter **W1** (574), to Wil, summer or autumn 1887. We will return to it in Chapter 7.

religion, religious thoughts still came to him during his attacks and brought him consolation.[17] The rumour of Tolstoy's book *My Religion* greatly appealed to him, less for its denial of any afterlife and more for its advocacy of faith without any cruelty. Vincent hoped to find in this a religion that would not increase human suffering, but instead bring consolation, courage, serenity and energy among other good things.[18]

There was an ominous moment in the November of 1889, when it seemed he would never start his Good Samaritan; he wrote to Theo stating very clearly that there was no question of him ever painting a biblical scene.[19] The storm that prompted him to say this then passed and his version is astonishing and, in my opinion, far superior to Delacroix's original.

His other biblical scenes are mostly concerned with Christ: a version of Rembrandt's 'The Raising of Lazarus' and various Sowers, after Millet and course Delacroix's 'Pietà', which started this new phase of copying. These provide further evidence for the line he drew between Christ and the rest of the Bible. In a letter to a fellow artist, Émile Bernard, he created the following analogy, comparing Christ in the Bible to a stone in the middle of a sour fruit:

> '… the consolation of that deeply saddening Bible, which rouses our despair and our indignation – which grieves us and utterly outrages us with its pettiness and contagious stupidity – the consolation is that – contained within, like a sweet nut within a hard shell or a bitter pulp – is Christ.'
>
> Letter **B8** (632), to Bernard 23/6/1888

If this denouncement of the Bible sounds excessively harsh, perhaps we could hear less the rhetoric and more the pain.

---

[17] Letter **605** (801), to Theo 7 or 8/9/1889.

[18] Letter **542** (686), to Theo 24/9/1888 and Letter **543** (687), to Theo 28/9/1888.

[19] Letter **615** (823), to Theo 21/11/1889.

Clearly something devastating happened that took him from a postulant minister to one who refused to accompany his parents into a church at Christmas.[20] We could also note how he communicated, illustrating his points by creating analogies.

Jesus' parables and van Gogh's analogies

Van Gogh often devised analogies to explain his views as clearly as possible. He wanted and needed to be understood, especially by those he loved. Often he drew his examples from the natural world or from rural life. His letters might seem somewhat cluttered by extraneous comments; after all, he often wrote in haste, in brief moments snatched from painting, never imagining an audience beyond the addressee. His analogies within these letters give remarkable insights into his own thinking. For instance, he wrote to Theo, likening his unappreciated talents to a warming fire:

> 'Someone might have a bright fire burning in his soul and no one comes by to warm themselves and all that passers-by notice is a wisp of smoke leaving the chimney before continuing on their way.'
> Letter **133** (155), to Theo around 24/6/1880

Later he tried to explain to Theo how falling in love had changed him, likening himself to a recently lit lamp:

> 'And love is something eternal, it may well change in aspect but not in its roots. And there is the same difference between someone who now loves and how he was before, as between a lamp that is lit and a lamp that isn't. The lamp was there and was a good lamp, but now it also gives light, as is its proper function. And one feels calmer about many things and gets better at the work he does.'
> Letter **276** (330), to Theo 21-28/3/1883

[20] Letter **166** (194), to Theo 29/12/1881.

Other examples of his analogies will crop up at points throughout this book. I find them both colourful and helpful as I seek to understand the man who painted with such passion.

Jesus was also keen to share his views with others and he too used his own form of analogies, better known to us as his 'parables'. He did not share van Gogh's need to explain himself with unambiguous clarity. Jesus tells his parables to create an enriching engagement with his audience. They are not exact line-for-line parallels. They are stories, packed with nuances that lead us to new places. Before they begin to yield their wisdom, they need to be entered and explored from within. His listeners must inhabit his narratives, asking with which characters they identify, finding none to be a perfect fit but all with something to say to them. Any who consider them 'nice stories', perhaps better suited for children, are missing out. If we engage properly, we will be changed. They provoke and confound even as they reassure. They defy reduction to any one-line summary. Whenever we attempt this, we strip them of their richness. They are designed to challenge and reshape our whole world view.

Some theologians of the early church approached them with rigid expectations, looking for just one single meaning at the cost of any others. Origen, writing in Alexandria in the third century, imagined a series of exact 'one for one' matches within the Good Samaritan. He saw it purely as a history of salvation and, in the process, excised from it any ethical guidance about what to do with a stranger in crisis:

'The man who was going down is Adam. Jerusalem is paradise, and Jericho is the world. The robbers are hostile powers. The Priest is the Law, the Levite is the prophets, and the Samaritan is Christ. The wounds are disobedience, the beast is the Lord's body, the inn, which accepts all who wish to enter, is the Church. ... The manager of the inn is the head of the Church, to whom its care has been entrusted.

And the fact that the Samaritan promises he will return represents the Saviour's second coming.'

Origen, Homilies 34:3

Augustine takes this even further:

> 'The binding of the wounds is the restraint of sin. Oil is the comfort of good hope; wine the exhortation to work with fervent spirit. ... The two pence are either the two precepts of love, or the promise of this life and of that which is to come.'

Augustine, *Quaestiones Evangeliorum,* II, 19

On the one hand, they are at liberty to interpret as they see fit. On the other, they will need to do some extra work to explain how this relates to the lawyer's question. Remember that Jesus tells this story as part of a conversation about ethics and eternity, not as some abstracted pronouncement or mission statement. Even so, it is not always obvious why Jesus deems his stories to be suitable responses to a question. On another occasion, Jesus' disciples ask him why he speaks in parables. We should not be overly surprised that his response seems wilfully mysterious:

> 'The reason I speak to them in parables is that "seeing they do not perceive, and hearing they do not listen, nor do they understand."'

Matthew 13:13

Jesus' parables are therefore quite different from van Gogh's analogies; the latter wanted his addressees to see his point and agree with him, so much so he often wove the explanation into his narrative.

Jesus seems content if his audience walk away, initially baffled. The Good Samaritan, as an answer, runs at a considerable tangent from the lawyer's original question; he asks about eternal life, Jesus gives him a story about exceptional kindness and an instruction to 'Go and do likewise'. If this lawyer listens carefully he will find an answer to a much better question, one that he does not ask. He might find that the Priest, the Levite, the Samaritan and even the wounded man – maybe especially the wounded man, all have crucial relevance for his life, now and for all eternity. He might even realise that this parable tells, not only his story, but also God's story; a theme to which we will return in the final chapter.

How Jesus copied and developed his own material

The Parable of the Good Samaritan appears just once in the Gospels. We cannot conclude from this that Jesus told this story only on this one occasion. It probably formed part of his repertoire, maybe even becoming as expected as 'Satisfaction' at a Rolling Stones concert. Over time and with retelling, his stories evolve. Jesus polishes, refines, adapts and expands his own material. In Matthew's Gospel, he tells a short parable about a father with two less-than-cooperative sons:

> 'A man had two sons; he went to the first and said, "Son, go and work in the vineyard today." He answered, "I will not"; but later he changed his mind and went. The father went to the second and said the same; and he answered, "I go, sir"; but he did not go. Which of the two did the will of his father?'
>
> Matthew 21:28-31

In this we see the same themes that find a much fuller expression in the Parable of the Prodigal Son in Luke's Gospel.[21] In like manner, we find in Luke Chapter 18 an alternative version of the exchange that precedes his telling of the Good Samaritan.[22]

---

[21] Luke 15:11-32.
[22] Luke 18:18-27. See also Matthew 19:16-22 and Mark 10:17-22.

A rich ruler asks him exactly the same question as the lawyer, 'Good Teacher, what must I do to inherit eternal life?'. Both conversations move to a summary of the commandments. Jesus then gives to both enquirers an instruction that is very hard to fulfil. The rich ruler is required to sell all his possessions and give to those in need. The lawyer is given the example of the Good Samaritan and told to go and do likewise.

My plan for this book is to explore some of the many meanings of this parable through the twin lenses of Vincent van Gogh's painting and his life. For now, can I simply emphasise two things?

1. The extremely difficult nature of both of Jesus' instructions: selling *everything* and caring for *everyone* in need.

2. These different instructions are given in answer to the same question, about inheriting eternal life.

Vincent van Gogh's thoughts on eternal life

Van Gogh also spent some time pondering eternity. In 1877, while still in his religious phase, his letters to Theo brimmed with confidence:

> 'There is something better than the glory of the worldly things; it is the feeling when our hearts burn within us on hearing His word, that is faith in God, love for Christ, belief in immortality – in a life after this life.'
>
> Letter **89** (109), to Theo 22/3/1877

When these simple reassurances no longer satisfied Vincent, the questions still remained. He found himself unable to countenance death as being an absolute end. In 1888, following the death of Anton Mauve, his former mentor, he wrote to his sister Wil. He was struggling to conceive how one who had so penetrated the core of life, could disappear so completely and utterly. What sort of afterlife existed for Mauve, he did not know, and he refused to speculate. He put his thoughts into an analogy, illustrating the futility of humans contemplating eternity by likening us to the grubs and bugs of the earth:

'Now I know that it is pretty much impossible for white potato or salad grubs, which later change into cockchafers, to be able to construct any meaningful concepts about a future existence above the ground. And it would be ill advised for them for them to undertake above ground investigations into this matter, the gardener or someone else interested in lettuce and vegetables would see them as harmful bugs and quickly and simply squash them.

'And for parallel reasons, I have little faith in the accuracy of our human concepts about the life to come. We can no more judge our own metamorphoses, without being prejudiced or over-hasty, than the white salad grubs can judge theirs.

'For the same reason that a salad grub ought to eat salad roots for its higher progression, so I think a painter ought to make paintings – and maybe there is something else afterwards.'

Letter **W2** (579), to Wil c. 28/2/1888

This analogy is one of my favourites. I enjoy the way van Gogh approaches lofty speculations about the afterlife through the earthiness of salad grubs. Jesus also brings questions of eternity down to ground level, with a man left for dead in the gutter of the road which runs down from Jerusalem to Jericho.

CHAPTER 2

The Road from Jerusalem to Jericho

A man was going down from Jerusalem to Jericho ...'

Luke 10:30

Van Gogh's painting

Take a good look at van Gogh's painting. Then in your mind's eye try to erase all the characters, including the mule, and see what is left to you: a wild, rocky land with a distinct emphasis on the vertical. To the left there is a wall of rock, towering far beyond the picture's frame. To the right there are more cliffs and also a cascade of water. At the top, in the middle, is a small inverted triangle of sky. Odd dabs of darker colour suggest the sort of scrubby plants that cling to such steep faces. But for the most part the far background is all painted in a distant blue.

31

Van Gogh begins this road with bold, left-leaning ochre strokes. Only the chilly mountain stream is painted with horizontals. So the eye is drawn ever upwards, following the road's course, switching to right-leaning strokes as it winds, cutting through the rougher greenish yellow of the mid-ground.

The road is narrow. Just to one side lies the Samaritan's travelling trunk where it was thrown open and then discarded as soon as its useful contents had been removed. It tilts at an alarming angle, marking the rocks at the edge of the walkable space.

There are no ruts in the road to suggest that carts might travel this way. Were it wide enough, it would still be too rough. Anything that needs transporting must be carried by hand or strapped to the back of a pack animal.

This is more the valley of the shadow of death than the place of green pastures and still waters. In this inhospitable gorge, the road is the safest place to be but, even so, it is not somewhere to linger. Van Gogh's message seems to be, 'keep to the road and keep moving'.

The actual road through the Judean wilderness

Vincent van Gogh never travelled further south than France or further east than the Netherlands. Instead he looked to Delacroix's lithograph on his wall. His preference was to paint from life but a trip to the Holy Land was beyond his means. He therefore never saw this road or walked its seventeen-mile length and three thousand, four hundred-foot descent from Jerusalem to Jericho.

As Jesus begins his story, the very mention of this road alerts his first audience to the likelihood of something bad happening. If a contemporary storyteller began, *'So this wealthy Danish couple decided to sail their expensive yacht down the coast of Somalia ...'* we would expect pirates to appear sooner or later. This road suffered a similar notoriety.

It was still a haunt of robbers in van Gogh's own lifetime. In 1859, the American missionary W. M. Thomson wrote about one of his earlier journeys on this road:

> '[We] prepared ourselves to descend, for as you remember that we must go, "*down* to Jericho." And sure enough, *down*, *down* we did go, over slippery rock, for more than a mile, then the path became less precipitous. Still, however the road follows the dry channel of a brook for several miles farther, as if descending into the very bowels of the earth. How admirably calculated for "robbers"!
>
> After leaving the brook, which turns aside too far to the south, we ascended and descended naked hills for several miles, the prospect gradually becoming more and more gloomy. Not a house, not even a tree, is to be seen; ...
> Not far from here, in a narrow defile, an English traveller was attacked, shot and robbed in 1820.'[23]

By the time the Reverend Dr Martin Luther King, Jr. visited the Holy Land with his wife in the 1960s, a more substantial road had been built, but nevertheless it still evoked the dangers Jesus described. They drove their hired car from Jerusalem, remarking how conducive the landscape would be for any robbers with ill intent. He recounted this journey in a sermon, claiming that in Jesus' time the road was known as, 'the Bloody Pass'.[24]

Jesus' first audiences are familiar with certain conventions regarding this, 'Bloody Pass'. They know for instance, that it is vital to seek as much information as possible both before and during the journey. The key questions are, *'Has there been any trouble lately?'* and *'Who else has passed by today?'*. All travellers

[23] *The Land and the Book, Volume 2*, W. M. Thomson, page 443, Harper & Brothers, New York 1860.

[24] 'I've Been to the Mountaintop', Dr Martin Luther King, Jr. A sermon preached on 3 April 1968, Mason Temple (Church of God in Christ Headquarters), Memphis, Tennessee.

ask these at the start of the road, and again whenever they pass anyone coming the other way.

Assuming the Samaritan also starts from Jerusalem and is heading down to Jericho (we are not told about *his* direction), we can be sure that he is aware of the others who are already ahead of him. Someone up at the top said something like, *'You're the fourth this morning; another fellow, then a Priest, and then a Levite set out before you. Good luck. Stay safe.'* If he is travelling up from Jericho, he would pass first the Priest and then the Levite before finding the wounded man.

The road offers another way of learning who else is journeying. With its twists and bends, it allows a traveller to see others considerably further along its winding length. This will be especially important when we come to the Levite. His choice to stop or pass on by has in part been made by the Priest, if the Levite takes his lead from him.

Jesus's audience have all this information before he begins. From the moment he mentions the road going down from Jerusalem to Jericho, they are ready for a drama to unfold.

Van Gogh's 'road' (or career)

Vincent van Gogh's road through life initially looked reasonably straightforward. His parents had no cause to foresee anything dramatic ahead. As we saw in Chapter 1, their eldest was due to follow his father into the ministry. However, his first job was with the art dealers, Goupil & Cie. His Uncle Vincent, or Uncle Cent as he was known within the family, worked there. He secured a post in the Hague for his sixteen-year-old nephew. This was never meant to be a long career for the young Vincent. Besides, his heart simply was not in it. His passionate nature could not be held by anything less than his destiny, although quite what this destiny was, remained to be discovered.

Vincent, at the age of twenty-two, used a telling phrase in a letter to Theo. He stated that neither he nor his sister Anna had yet found their true selves and as such they were lagging a long way behind the imposing figure of their father:

> '... we're lacking in solidity and simplicity and sincerity, one cannot become *simple* and true in a flash.'
>
> Letter **43** (056), to Theo 14/10/1875

Unfortunately this passion for simplicity and truth did not embrace any notion of well-being. Vincent's quest to be true to his vocation did great damage to both his physical and his mental health. As both evangelist and painter, he neglected his basic human needs. He often did not eat properly. He worked relentlessly, shunning rest and pushing himself onwards to reach some ever-escalating point of attainment. In 1882 he explained to Theo how he had managed to produce a large number of studies in a very short time. He claimed to have worked unceasingly, barely taking time off to eat or drink.[25] His mantra of 'soundness and simplicity and sincerity' would have benefitted immensely from the addition of 'self-care'.

By the time he parted company with Goupil & Cie, he was immersing himself deeply in the Bible, having become convinced that his vocation was to preach the Gospel. This path turned out to be a dead end and, after the painful episodes outlined in Chapter 1, he accepted that full-time Christian service was not for him.

His sense of vocation however remained intact. In many ways he kept the old box marked 'vocation' now emptied of its Christian contents and simply filled it afresh with a new career, that of an artist. Arguably these two very different contents required two very different boxes. Vincent however did not make any such accommodation. In his early days as an artist his structures and his rather extreme expectations

---

[25] Letter **227** (258), to Theo 20/8/1882.

were almost identical to those of his religious phase. He says as much to Theo, lumping artists and evangelists together:

'But I must continue pursuing the path I am currently on; if I do nothing, if I don't study, if I stop trying, then I am doomed and woe is me. This is how I see things – keep on keeping on, that's what I must do.

But what is your actual goal, you ask. This goal does become clearer; it draws itself slowly and surely, just as the sketch becomes the drawing which becomes the picture; it's only as gradually you work ever more seriously, as you keep digging ever deeper – that an initially ill-defined concept, that first elusive, fleeting thought, gets pinned down.

You have to understand that what's true for evangelists, is the same for artists.'

Letter **133** (155), to Theo 22 & 24/7/1880

There are some clues as to what he thought the goal of his new vocation might look like. He told Theo that he wanted his work to touch people. He sought that point where his work would reveal what was in his heart:

'What I want & what I aim for is blindingly difficult and yet I don't believe I'm aiming too high. I want to do drawings which will have an impact on some people.

...

In short, I want to reach the point where people say of my work, this man has deep feelings and this man understands subtlety.'

Letter **218** (249), to Theo 21/7/1882

He drove himself incredibly hard, often comparing his vocation to the back-breaking work of the farm labourers whom he drew and later painted. He wrote as if he was not in control and it was his vocation that called all the shots, with scant regard for his well-being:

> 'Art is jealous, she won't accept second place to any illness, so I give in to her demands. People like me aren't actually allowed to be sick.
>
> …
>
> Art demands relentless work – work despite anything else and always constant observation. By relentless I mean, first and foremost a continuous labour, but also never abandoning one's views, whatever anyone else says.'
>
> Letter **218** (249), to Theo 21/7/1882

This 'relentless work' left very little space for love in his life. He was often lonely and pined for a wife and a family, but his ultra-demanding sense of vocation granted him very few concessions. Even in 1888, several years after abandoning the Church and two years before his death, he still viewed his life in religious, monastic terms. He wrote to his friend, Émile Bernard offering advice about how an artist lives:

> '… you've got to forge your character so it becomes hard as nails – character that'll see you well into old age – you've got to live like a monk who visits the brothel once a fortnight – that's what I do, it's not terribly poetic – but after all, I feel my duty is to subordinate my life to painting.'
>
> Letter **B8** (632), to Bernard 23/6/1888

This is not sound advice for a prospective priest or for an artist. Our deeper human needs cannot be so neatly sheared away from our wider lives, to be dealt with as economically and efficiently as regular haircuts. In the end he viewed sex as a distraction from his vocation. Like the hunger for food, its demands had to be sated but he regretted the cost, which was not merely financial but also detrimental to his art. He was even less poetic in another letter to Bernard:

> 'Painting and a lot of fucking just don't work together; the brain becomes mushy. And how bloody annoying that is!'
>
> Letter **B7** (628), to Bernard 18/6/1888

Vincent continued at his vocation despite a crushing concern: the realisation that he would never be able to return Theo's investment. He had set out expecting that one day his work would sell, he would then be able to sustain himself and repay Theo. The popular myth says that he never sold anything. In truth, he sold several drawings and one canvas but the income from these was nowhere near sufficient to cover his costs.

We know how the artistic road continued after his life had ended. There is the overwhelming irony that his paintings now sell for millions upon millions. In 1990, exactly one hundred years after his death, his portrait of Dr Gachet was bought at auction for an incredible 82.5 million USD. His works rarely go on sale. Instead they fill the star places in museums around the world. In Amsterdam there is an entire museum dedicated to his work. He visited the Rijksmuseum in 1885, never guessing that an equally popular museum, dedicated entirely to his work and bearing his name, would one day be built next door. Near Arnhem, the Kröller-Müller Museum houses the second largest collection of his works, including his Good Samaritan. Back in 1888 he had no notion of the cultural and financial excitement his name would one day cause. He did however understand how the art markets failed to value living painters. With uncanny prescience, he wrote the following to his sister Wil:

> 'People pay a lot of money for a painter's work once he is dead. And they undervalue living painters: they 'dead-end'

us with the work of those who are no longer with us.'[26]

Letter W4 (626), to Wil 22/6/1888

Tragically, with less than a year of life remaining, he wrote to Theo from the asylum at Saint-Rémy, speaking of his sense of failure. The goal, which he had once hoped would reveal itself, if only he fully committed himself to his vocation, remained as ill-defined and as elusive as ever. Note his use of past and future tenses, perhaps signalling some awareness that his end might be nearing him:

> 'To succeed, to find lasting prosperity, requires a different sort of character than mine; I'll never do what I could have done....'

Letter 605 (801), to Theo 7 or 8/9/1889

Another great irony is that at the time of writing this, he had recently finished some of his best-known works; his 'Irises' and his 'Starry Night'. In his remaining eleven months, he would go on to produce his 'Bedroom at Arles' and over one hundred and seventy further canvases, including his Good Samaritan. He worked as one possessed, sensing an approaching but unpredictable deadline. He offered Theo an analogy to explain the pressure he felt, comparing himself to a miner:

> 'As for myself, my health is good at the moment – I think M. Peyron is right in saying that I am not truly mad, since my thinking is absolutely normal and clear in the times between [the attacks] and even more so than before. But

---

[26] This rather clumsy sentence in English comes from a rather clumsy sentence in the original Dutch, hampered by the problem of how to translate the word 'doodslaander' (literally 'deathslaying') which is recognised neither by modern Dutch dictionaries nor by my Dutch friend Charl, who helped me with the translations.

during the attacks however, it is terrible, so much so that I have no idea at all what's going on. But all this presses me onwards, to work and to seriousness. I'm like a coal miner who's in constant danger and so works in haste.'

Letter **610** (810), to Theo 8/10/1889

These 'attacks' were the episodes when he became confused and lost his grasp on normality. They were very frightening. It was during the first serious attack, in December 1888, that he took a razor to his ear, cut it off and delivered it to a woman, Rachel, who worked in one of the local brothels.[27] Following this he was convinced that more attacks would come and a single truly violent attack would rob him of his ability to paint. He worked therefore like a miner in an unstable mineshaft, frantically hewing as much coal as he possibly could before the roof collapsed, so frightened was he of an existence where he was unable to paint.

Vincent van Gogh's road through life was never an easy stroll. He understood this by the time he was twenty-eight and falling in love for a second time. He viewed those who 'sold out' to greed and ambition as making straight, steady but ultimately unsatisfying progress. This could never be his way. He was determined to pursue his vocation, erring always on the side of love. He foresaw his way was hazardous but always far more worthwhile. In 1881, he explained this to Theo in an analogy that compares life and its passions to a ship with two different sails:

'The passions are the sails of a little ship, you understand. And someone, aged twenty, who surrenders himself

[27] There has been much discussion over the years as to whether he cut off his ear lobe or the whole ear. Bernadette Murphy has tracked down previously hidden documents that point convincingly to it being the whole ear (Chapter 14, 'Unlocking the Events', *Van Gogh's Ear*, Bernadette Murphy, Vintage 2017).

completely to his feeling, will catch too much wind, and his boat then fills with water and – and he perishes – or he comes back up again. On the other hand, someone who hoists up his mast only the one sail, Ambition & Co. and nothing else, sails straight through life without mishap, without lurching until – until finally something happens that makes him realise, "I don't have enough sail." Then he says, "Everything, everything that I have, I would freely give for one square meter more of sail and I don't have it." He falls into despair.

Ah! But now he recalls that he possesses another resource – he thinks of the sail called "love" which until now was despised and stowed away with the ballast. And this sail saves him. The sail "love" must save him, and if he doesn't hoist it, he'll never arrive.

The first case, that of the man whose boat capsized when he was twenty or thereabouts and then sank. Or did it? No. That boat has recently reappeared on the surface – and is that of your brother V who's writing to you as one "'"who has been down but yet came up again".'

Letter **157** (183), to Theo 12 / 11 / 1881

It is a great sadness that despite these fine intentions, Vincent did not experience the love he craved. When he wrote this analogy in 1881 he fully expected love to be central to his life. He had just fallen hard for Kee Vos, of whom we will hear more in the next chapter. He was still idealistic, hoping his vocation would exceed simply creating art. Painting well not enough for him, he had to *be,* as well as to *do*: to *be* the passionate, sincere, sound and simple-living soul that he saw as his true self. He also believed, aged twenty-eight and still with the buoyancy of youth, that even after capsizing, he could resurface and continue. With hindsight, we can see that he never hoisted the sail of greedy ambition, and he never compromised his vision in order to produce work purely for money. Tragically he was never to sail successfully with love. This left him with a third sail, which he did not include in his analogy. This sail might be called 'the ravenous desire to paint and to keep on painting, regardless of any personal cost'. Sadly, as he aged, he journeyed increasingly under this sail alone, even to the point of shipwreck.

Some further thoughts arising from
The Road

Vocation

Vocation can be a tricky subject. How do we know when to hoist which sails on our ship, and which combinations will best serve us? Can we ever speak with any certainty about a destination? And if so, do we aim for it or do we trust the winds to take us there? Does God have a pre-set plan for us? If so, what will happen when we inevitably take a wrong turn? How can we be sure that the path we currently pursue is the one God has chosen for us and not just something that we wanted for ourselves? There are probably as many answers as there are people asking these questions. The most famous quotation from Shakespeare's *Twelfth Night* identifies three groupings:

> 'Some are born great, some achieve greatness, and some have greatness thrust upon 'em.'
>
> *Twelfth Night*, Act 2 Scene V

Van Gogh falls squarely into the second category. He became one of the world's most recognised artists by his achievement: his paintings. We might argue that he was born with an innate talent but unlike Mozart, he showed very few signs at an early age. He achieved his greatness through his unstinting commitment to capturing in paint his vision of life, even if that meant kneeling in mud [28] or battling that 'spiteful, whining wind', the Mistral.[29]

Not everyone has the kind of mind that considers 'vocation'

---

[28] Letter **227** (258), to Theo 20/8/1882.
[29] Letter **B7** (628), to Bernard 18/6/1888.

in the first place. Some people never ask such questions, others only at certain points in life, for instance when contemplating career options, during a mid-life crisis or at the start of retirement. The type who actively seek out a vocation usually imagine something dramatic, possibly even Damascene; the revelation of a new, all-consuming focus to their lives.

Perhaps it is only with hindsight that many of us gain any sense of our vocations; very few of us know exactly what we are born to and what we can achieve. None can predict how the actions of others will affect us. If Jesus were to tell a parable about our lives, we would prefer him to begin, 'A sower went out to sow, and his seed fell on good soil' rather than 'This person set out from Jerusalem to Jericho ...'

Some good vocations are squeezed out of existence before they can ever be properly acknowledged, maybe even before they can be consciously sensed. Over the past two thousand years, how many women never fulfilled their God-given vocation to be a priest or a bishop, because they lived among the weeds of patriarchy, which strangled and choked their potential? Van Gogh was a white, well-educated, European male who came from a relatively affluent family. He certainly suffered in the pursuit of his vocation; no one could say his road was easy, but it was at least possible. Imagine a Dutch woman, born at the same time in the neighbouring village, with similar gifts and drive but from a much poorer family. She never had the 'luxury', however dubious, of 'abandoning it all' to pursue her passion. The barriers restricting her were too immense.

Does everyone have a pre-set, God-given path to walk?

If we understand vocation as a call from God, to be our best authentic selves, then yes, we might say that everyone has a God-given path. 'Vocation' however is often used to describe the careers of artists, medics, politicians, celebrities or clerics, who have abandoned a safe path for a much riskier one.

The Road from Jerusalem to Jericho

We cannot all lead lives of fame. In the musical *The Book of Mormon*, Elder Kevin Price, one of the lead characters, is convinced that he is destined to do 'something incredible' with his life. He plans to make his life so spectacular that it will 'blow God's freaking mind'! He can never be 'normal'; God has selected him from millions to be outstanding and he intends to surpass even this![30]

But who is to say what 'normal' is? The same thing can appear as unremarkable to one person and astonishing to the next. To the uninformed, a forest is a clump of trees. To the naturalist, it is a fascinating collision of worlds; a warzone where different species battle against each other for light and water. It is also a place of wonderful balance, where animals and plants live interdependently with each other, the casual waste of one being life itself to another. It is a great privilege to hear an expert open the door to these mysteries. In the same way, God sees all human life, and no life lived is unremarkable to God. Any hierarchy of vocations is a purely human concoction. Who is to say that any authentic path is not a vocation in God's eyes?

But how do those with a sense of vocation know they still are 'on track'? Again, hindsight will be our greatest help with this; I have come to believe that God does not lay out our lives before us with clear maps. Rather, God gives us life as a gift to explore. We are not left without guidance; Jesus, when talking about helpful and less than helpful guides, says:

> 'You will know them by their fruits. Are grapes gathered from thorns, or figs from thistles?'
>
> Matthew 7:16

We can apply this thinking to vocations. A healthy track ought to feel right – not at all times but certainly in times of consolation.

[30] See the songs 'You and Me (But Mostly Me)', 'I Believe' and 'All American Prophet' from the musical, *The Book of Mormon* - Trey Parker, Matt Stone and Robert Lopez.

This does not mean that our path will be endlessly smooth but the fruit of being on a good path will be some strength inside of us, compelling us to carry on despite the obstacles put in our way. A wrong path will yield no such fruit; it will always feel like a slog. There may be some rewards along the way but these will not satisfy.

After his major false start of seeking to be a minister, Vincent settled onto his new road. He met many detractors and discouragers there. The fruits of his vocation could not be measured in sales, or success with galleries, at least not in his lifetime. However, something inside of him refused to give in. He continually found his sense of rightness at the easel, where his other concerns melted away.

We can also apply Jesus' teaching about fruits to *how* a vocation is worked out. Hindsight, along with the galleries and the million-dollar prices tags, confirms that van Gogh certainly did have a vocation to paint. The fruits of *how* he set about fulfilling this are less appealing. He chose to walk his path almost as a slave, pouring out his life like a religious offering, surrendering himself to its unrelenting demands, whilst denying himself comfort, rest and proper sustenance. He ended his association with organised religion largely for the way it handled love. It is sadly ironic that, having ditched one vocation, ostensibly for love, he then pursued another with such vigour that he was still unable to find love. Perhaps we can only call a vocation 'good' when not just its end, but also its pursuit is commendable. Otherwise an end might be offered as the justification of some ghastly means.

Caring for self

In Vincent's letters he often wrote as the wise elder brother, passing on nurturing insights to Theo and Wil. We find him as a minister, wanting to be the provider, rather than the recipient of care. This creates an imbalance, which taken to an extreme becomes both patronising to others and dangerous to self. Severe, chronic self-neglect is a sure sign of a vocation gone wrong.

In the conversation immediately preceding the Parable of the Good Samaritan, Jesus approves a version of the greatest commandment that is actually three commandments in one. The order is important. We are to love God and also to love our neighbour. The third part is implicit, appearing in the two words 'as yourself'. It therefore has the same priority as the second. If we refuse our duty to love ourselves, then we are likely to become a burden to those we initially sought to serve. Burn-out might occasionally look heroic but it is no sign of success. Those who snort with derision or roll their eyes when Jesus speaks of his yoke being easy need to revisit how they are fulfilling their vocation.

Assessing how well a vocation is going

How do we assess whether we are truly fulfilling our vocation? Should we look for an uninterrupted stream of productive days? Or should we expect very little apart from the occasional flash of brilliance? I found it much easier to count a working day as 'well-spent' when I belonged to a large company and wore a uniform. As a vicar, and now that I'm self-employed, I find it much harder to judge how well I am using my time. Van Gogh had his own version of this anxiety. In his early days as a painter, he saw himself as a student learning his craft through endless sketching. If by evening he had created a large stack of work or mastered a tricky perspective or discovered some breakthrough in figure drawing, he might declare that he had had a good day. Later on he expected his work to sell. He responded to his lack of commercial success by working ever harder, sometimes painting two new canvases a day.

I have a theory that we spend relatively little time doing the one thing that defines us. I developed this theory as an unenthusiastic adult in a ski school. I observed that a skiing holiday requires a great many things before and after the main attraction – the act of safely sliding down a mountain. Each skiing day is made up of locating all the necessary clobber, wrapping up warmly, squeezing feet into unyielding boots, hobbling to the lifts, queuing at both bottom and top, until finally the actual skiing begins. It does not last for long. It takes far less time to slide down than it does to return to the top, even without the queuing. Then there are the breaks for elevenses, lunch and glühwein. All too soon, the short winter day ends. The light becomes flat, making the final run home that bit more dangerous. By four o'clock it is tea-time back in the chalet. The total amount of time spent actually sliding downwards is minimal. In the same way, a painter's day might contain only a few short moments with brush in hand. There are any number of distractions from this core task: marketing, accounting, paying taxes, posting images on social media, chatting to customers, shopping for supplies, negotiating with galleries, mounting, framing, packaging, mailing work out and then locating items lost in the post, and so on. Whole days can be swallowed by all this stuff which is not painting, but which nevertheless is part and parcel of a painter's life. The same frustrations can be found in other vocations: teachers spend too long on paperwork and nurses find their time with patients eroded by management meetings.

Vincent enjoyed analogies taken from the natural world. I wonder if he ever noticed how much time a butterfly spends being a butterfly? The answer is relatively little, once all the caterpillar and cocoon phases have been factored in. This type of reflection might have helped him address his dangerously high expectations of himself and replace them with something more realistic.

At the end of the road ...

Each road comes to an end. People of faith believe that after death we will arrive at that moment of ultimate hindsight and discover how well we have spent our days. Elder Kevin Price fully expects his Heavenly Father to tell him he's done an 'awesome job' and give him his own planet. St Paul awarded himself this assessment:

'I have fought the good fight, I have finished the race, I have kept the faith. From now on there is reserved for me the crown of righteousness.'

1 Timothy 4:7-8a

Other Christians look to Jesus' parables and hope God will say to them:

'Well done, good and faithful servant ... Enter into the joy of your lord.'

Matthew 25:21 (NKJV)

I remain inspired by an elderly woman. Towards the very end of an incredible life, she reviewed her many achievements. She had never appeared in the press nor won any awards. She had lived abroad in her childhood and then settled in England, where she married and raised her family. She underwent the most agonising of bereavements. She survived cancer and then supported other cancer sufferers. She genuinely radiated life, good sense, fun, generosity and hospitality wherever she went. Her many acts of kindness were much appreciated by their recipients, but elsewhere in the wider world, they went unremarked. She won no medals and desired none. Near to the very end of her life, she wrote a simple note – a line of eight words to say what had really mattered to her in her eighty-eight years. She tucked it away in a place where her children were likely to find it. It read simply:

'I have loved and I have been loved.'

For her, this was summary enough. Her life had been filled with love and as such her vocation as a human was fulfilled. She would never have claimed any title such as 'Good Samaritan' but in understanding the importance of love, she certainly did not walk life's road with the same blinkers or hasty footsteps of either the Priest or the Levite in Jesus' story.

CHAPTER 3

The Wounded Man and The Robbers

'A man was going down from Jerusalem to Jericho,
and fell into the hands of robbers,
who stripped him, beat him, and went away,
leaving him half dead.'

Luke 10:30

Van Gogh's painting

Van Gogh's wounded man appears all but lifeless. He has been savagely assaulted and then left for dead by the roadside. In the moment caught by the picture he is contributing nothing at all to his rescue. All the effort comes from another man who struggles alone to heave him up onto the back of his animal. In his current condition a stretcher would be far more appropriate, but neither this nor an ambulance, nor even a cart is available on this narrow, lonely track.

The wounded man's face remains slack, his mouth downturned in so wretched a way that it could almost appear scornful. But he is feeling no such thing. He is unlikely to be conscious of any thought or emotion. His eyes are either half-open or deeply sunk or heavily bruised. They are painted with such thick brushstrokes it is hard to tell.

His head is raised which might be a sign of some returning awareness. Perhaps he is groggily coming to. It might equally be the moment where, at the Samaritan's heft, his neck has jerked backwards, rolling his head upwards, only for his chin to thump back down on to his chest a moment later.

His hands are twisted and swollen, like those of one who has been tortured. This might be intentional, adding to the severity of the beating meted out by the robbers. Delacroix draws these hands with much more precision and in a way that suggests a degree of cooperation between the wounded man and the Samaritan. Van Gogh however sometimes struggled with hands. He complained to Theo about their difficulty in a letter after his other attempt at copying a Delacroix, 'Pietà'.[31] It might simply be that he rushed these, focusing on other aspects of the work and never returning to tidy them later.

Jesus has told us that the wounded man was stripped of his clothes. To protect his modesty, van Gogh, like Delacroix has provided him with a cloak wrapped around his midriff. We could say that, according to the painting, it was the Good Samaritan himself who provides this cloak. Remember that van Gogh copied a black and white lithograph and was therefore free to choose his own colours. A quick internet search shows us that Delacroix clothed the wounded man in light brown material, the same colour as sackcloth. In van Gogh's version, the man's covering

---

[31] Letter **605** (801), to Theo 7 or 8/9/1889, see also picture F 630, JH 1775.

exactly matches the blue of his rescuer's trousers, suggesting that the Samaritan wrapped him in his own cloak. The wounded man's only other garment is a bandage around his head, not dissimilar from the bandage van Gogh himself wore after mutilating his ear.[32]

Van Gogh as the wounded man

Did van Gogh see himself in this wounded man? Sadly he did not record his thoughts as he painted this picture and so we are left to speculate. We are more familiar with van Gogh as a bearded man. However, in his final self-portrait of September 1889 he was clean-shaven.[33] Delacroix's wounded man has no beard, so this is not a deliberate change. But since van Gogh's wounded man was both bandaged and clean shaven, it seems likely that he would have thought of himself as he painted.

If the wounded man is, in some sense, a self-portrait, it is hardly flattering. But van Gogh understood he had long lost his youthful looks. Writing to Theo in 1888, he claimed that his appearance was 'extremely haggard', likening himself to the main character in Émile Wauters' painting 'The Madness of Hugo van der Goes'. He then suggests that, without a beard, he also resembles the priest, standing behind Hugo.[34] However flippantly he makes these comments, we can see that he was in the habit of identifying himself with figures in other artists' works and was even able to see more than one version of himself in the same picture. We might therefore argue that the bearded Samaritan resembled his younger, bearded self. Hold that thought. We will return to it later, in Chapter 7.

Van Gogh's wounded people

Who else might Vincent have thought about as he painted this wounded figure? There are many possible candidates. He

---

[32] See pictures F 529, JH 1658 'Self-Portrait with Bandaged Ear and Pipe' and F527, JH 1657 'Self-Portrait with Bandaged Ear'.

[33] F 252, JH 1665 Self-Portrait.

[34] Letter **514** (650), to Theo c. 25/7/1888.

devoted his life to observing those who lived hard lives. Here are some examples.

Hungry schoolboys

When he worked briefly in a boys' school in Ramsgate, he observed with pity the plight of disobedient boys who were deprived of their supper. He grieved that all the boys and not just the noisy ones shared in this punishment. He wrote to Theo:

> 'You should have seen them standing at the window and looking out. There was something melancholy about it; they have so little beyond their food and drink to look forward to and get them through one day to the next.'
>
> Letter **67** (83), to Theo 31/5/1876

Coal miners

As an evangelist in the Borinage, a mining region of Southern Belgium, he noted the harshness of everyday life:

> 'The labourers there are mostly folk emaciated and ashen through fever; they look weary and gaunt, weather-beaten and prematurely aged. Likewise the women are generally sallow and withered. All around the mine are shabby miners' dwellings along with a couple of dead trees – completely blackened by smoke, thorn-hedges, dunghills and ash heaps, mountains of unusable coal, etc.'
>
> Letter **129** (151), to Theo 4/1879

He went on in this letter to describe to Theo some of the individuals that he had met, including a miner badly wounded in a firedamp explosion.

Peasants

Vincent frequently wrote to Theo about his passion for drawing peasants, finding in them an authenticity lacking in his own family's more middle-class circles. The term 'peasants' is uneasy. Nowadays its use is mostly pejorative, evoking uncultured dim-wittedness rather than honest farm work. But Vincent never wrote about 'peasants' with anything other than deep respect, sometimes over-idealising their lives. When his letters are read with this in mind, his observations appear less as a Pulp pop parody[35] and more a revelation of his deep empathy.

A destitute woman

When Vincent saw a young pregnant woman, sick, desperate, and walking the streets in winter, he decided to act. She had been abandoned by her child's father and was now destitute. The woman was called Clasina Maria Hoornik, but Vincent knew her simply as 'Sien'.[36] There will be more about their relationship in just a moment.

A patient at the asylum

In early June 1889, a new patient arrived at the asylum in Saint-Rémy. He was extremely unwell and caused a considerable disturbance. Vincent himself had been there for less than a month. He wrote to Theo with no hint of annoyance at this individual's continual shouting, his destruction of straightjackets, his throwing of food or his noisy trashing of his bedroom. Vincent's only reactions were sadness for his sorry state, and admiration for the patience of the staff combined with optimism that their methods would eventually bring calmness to this poor man. He made no complaint; he simply recorded his observations before moving on to discuss paintings and how he had seen the morning star from his window, long before dawn. If it was this new patient who had caused him to be awake at this hour, he did not say.[37]

---

[35] See Pulp's 1995 song 'Common People'.
[36] Letter **192** (224), to Theo 3-12/5/1882.
[37] Letter **593** (777), to Theo between 31/5 and 6/6/1889.

Van Gogh's quest for love

Vincent was certainly a wounded soul. If he was reflecting on his love life as he painted, he surely would have recognised himself in the battered figure being gently shoved upwards onto the mule. His adventures in love contained a great deal of heartache and very few moments of happiness. What follows is a brief history of his quest for loving companionship.

His first love – Eugénie Loyer

Vincent was twenty years old and living in London. The previous year he might have had eyes for the pretty Caroline Haanebeek, but in 1873 he fell well and truly for his landlady's daughter, Eugénie Loyer. She was already secretly engaged and therefore rejected his proposal. At the time, Vincent took this badly. He found new lodgings and eventually left London altogether, for Paris. We have already heard about his anguish. In his analogy of the ship with two sails, Vincent referred to his twenty-year-old self capsizing, having let the sail 'love' catch too much wind. To recover, he sought refuge in religious mania. Eugénie cannot be blamed for this. The seeds were already there, just waiting for the right conditions to germinate and grow. As his religious phase drew to its close, his interest in romantic love resurfaced.

His major (and most catastrophic) love – Kee Vos

Vincent fell disastrously hard for his cousin Kee Vos ('Kee' being short for Katherine). He described his feelings to Theo, offering an older brother's insights into love:

'There are 3 stages.

1. Not loving and not being loved.
2. Loving and not being loved (the present case)
3. Loving and being loved

Now I tell you that the second stage is better than the first, but the third! That's the one!

Now, old boy, go and fall in love, and tell me about it sometime.'

Letter **153** (179), to Theo 3/11/1881

Kee had already rejected Vincent's suit before he wrote this. His upbeat cajoling of Theo indicates the depth of his denial. He even enjoyed stage 2, having convinced himself that stage 3 must surely follow. Kee had opted for the cruel-to-be-kind approach. She was so deep in her grief for her husband and so preoccupied with caring for their child, that at first she failed to notice Vincent's attentions. Once she was aware, she told him, 'No, never, ever'. These three words began to plague him as the hopes inherent within 'stage 2' began to wane. He poured out much angst and ink seeking to discover exactly what she was really saying in this 'No, never, ever'. Her meaning, which was plain enough, did not alter – she did not wish to marry him.

He found this rejection impossible to accept. One evening in December 1881 he arrived uninvited at her family's home on the Keizersgracht in Amsterdam and demanded to see her. He gave a full account of this visit to Theo, revealing an astonishing inability to imagine any perspective other than his own.[38] An alternative version can be easily constructed from his words alone. This would tell of a man, maddened by denial, pushing his way into a house and shouting the odds until kindness eventually calmed him. Despite recording these facts himself, Vincent seemed to find no fault in his behaviour. He was unable to see anything beyond his own sense of deepest betrayal. He was appalled that Kee's family had allowed her to leave by the back door before admitting him to the dining room. Clearly they had already steeled themselves for some sort of show-down with him. Kee's father had written a letter asking him to respect her wishes and desist. Having yet

[38] Letter **164** (193), to Theo 21/12/1881.

to send it and now finding Vincent before him, he read it out loud. Vincent's response was to parody his uncle's delivery. His uncle was a clergyman and it seemed obvious to Vincent that his many faults were attributable to his religious mind-set. He only conceded to his elderly aunt and uncle's kindness when they insisted on leaving their warm home for the cold muddy streets to find him a cheap hotel, for which they paid. He returned to them in the next couple of days, where once again they carefully explained that his suit was cold. Tragically this was not enough and Vincent remained resolutely stuck at 'stage 2', utterly unable to grasp why 'stage 3' was being delayed.

In a later letter to Theo, he describes an even more disturbing incident. This might be additional information about his December visit to Kee's house, or perhaps he was writing about a further visit. On arrival he insisted on seeing her, only to be told his persistence was 'sickening'. He was accused of trying to coerce her, which left him outraged. He then held his left hand over an oil lamp and repeated his demands. The lamp was extinguished and he left in shame. He claimed that soon after this his love for Kee had died within him, leaving an 'infinite void' in its place. He felt as worthless as if he had been in a slave market, utterly forsaken, just as Jesus had felt forsaken by God.[39] His feelings however did not disappear and he continued to churn over her three words, 'No, never, ever'.

As late as 1883, he was still struggling to come to terms with the pain of this rejection. He wrote to Theo:

'... nothing has changed in me, that it is and remains a wound, which I live with and carry ever in my depths and cannot heal. In years to come it will be what it was on the first day.

I hope that you understand what a struggle I've had within myself of late.'

Letter **313** (374), to Theo, 18/8/1883

---

[39] Letter **193** (228), to Theo 14/5/1882.

This whole incident rings several alarm bells. In today's terms, Vincent certainly harasses Kee and her family. Some might go further and accuse him of stalking her. In all this he is our main informant. He unwittingly indicts himself by his own narrative. He remained dangerously unaware that his love was only perceived as 'love' by him. No other player in this drama would name it thus. We should also be concerned that when he was faced with 'the void', he self-harmed. This is a trait that would resurface later in his life, as his mental health deteriorated.

His lengthy rebound – Sien Hoornik

Sien was *not* a rebound! Vincent is very clear with Theo that this was a 'moving on'. They met in the same winter that Kee rejected him. Their relationship almost tore Vincent from his family and from his mentors in the art world. As a sex worker, Sien was, in their estimation, an utterly unsuitable fiancée for either a minister's son or an artist. Vincent saw a woman in trouble; they saw a prostitute. Their judgement made him all the more determined to stick with her.

In May 1882 he wrote to Theo with more than an echo of the Good Samaritan, insisting that:

> '"Love they neighbour as thyself." is the A. B. C. of all morality.'
>
> Letter **198** (227), to Theo 14/5/1882

He filled many letters with arguments about how he could not and would not abandon Sien. He admitted that initially she had been an object of pity, before she became his model and then his lover. His passion however seemed to be less for her and more for the *rightness* of being with her. He became her martyr, her rescuer, a Good Samaritan to this wounded soul, found in the winter gutter. In so doing he was able to cock a snook at his father and other professional Christians. He was being Christ-like in his redemption of a fallen woman.[40] Through Sien, he was teaching them what genuine love looked like – and it had nothing in common with their 'Jesuitisms'. This is not to say he was cynically using Sien purely to score points. He did feel a genuine affection for her. He told Theo how they both fulfilled certain needs in each other:

> 'She [Sien] and I are two ill-fated people who keep each other company and bear the burden together and for that very reason the unhappiness turns into happiness and the unbearable becomes bearable.'
>
> Letter **204** (234), to Theo 1 or 2/6/1882

He found the simple act of drawing her helped him to overcome the wounds of Kee's rejection. She soothed him. She also provided him with the family life he had long craved. This made him so happy that at times he cried.[41]

The relationship did not last. His time with Sien was to be his only experience of living as a husband and father-figure. They never got around to marrying and, in the end, he was unable to remain with her. Her mother interfered, but blaming her might be too easy. Certainly Sien did not change as he had hoped she might; in his own words, she continued to be weak and slovenly.[42] Perhaps his family's gradual acceptance of his situation lessened his resolve to continue. Perhaps the foundations of their love, being pity, loneliness and a desire to rescue, were never likely to support a lasting edifice. They parted in 1883. He wrote the following to Theo in March

[40] He also drew inspiration from Zola's character, Madame François in *La Ventre de Paris*, who rescues an unconscious figure found lying in the gutter. She does this despite the jeers of bystanders. Van Gogh claimed this was the same 'true humanity' he was showing to Sien. See Letter **219** (250), to Theo 23/7/1882 .

[41] Letter **210** (224), to Theo 2/7/1882.

[42] Letter **324** (386), to Theo c. 15/9/1883.

1884. If this is a reflection on his relationship with Sien, it is hardly flattering:

> 'And as for myself – back in my salad days I told you plainly and clearly, that if I couldn't find a good woman, I'd take a bad one – better a bad woman than none at all.
>
> I know plenty of people who'd insist on the opposite and are as fearful of "children" as I am of "no children".
>
> As for myself – I don't easily abandon a principle even when something has failed many times.'
>
> Letter **386a** (474), to Theo 10/12/1884

Despite this further sadness, Vincent still clung to a dream of domestic bliss.

A short romance – Margot Begemann

He fell in love again fairly swiftly, this time with Margot Begemann, his neighbour in Neunen. He wrote to Theo, comparing himself to Octave Mouret, a character in Zola's *Au Bonheur des Dames*. Octave leaves his womanising past when he spots the humble, hardworking Denise Badhu. She is an unlikely match for him and resists his advances for a long time, despite her secret adoration for him. Octave spends most of the book in the delicious anguishes of 'stage 2' love, only reaping the rewards of 'stage 3' in the final paragraphs. Vincent's fantasy did not become a reality with Margot. Her sisters strongly opposed their union. She became overwhelmed by the stress of their resistance and tried to take her own life. Her name quickly ceased to appear in Vincent and Theo's letters.

His final romance – Agostina Segatori

Agostina was the Italian owner of Le Tambourin, a restaurant in Paris. The letters have very little to say about her simply because Theo and Vincent were living together and therefore had no need to write to each other. What can be gleaned about this time has none of the high drama of his love for Kee or even Sien. They were together from December 1886 to May 1887. There was certainly a business element to their relationship, since Vincent was allowed to display some of his work in Le Tambourin. Afterwards he wrote to Theo that he suspected her miscarriage had been, in truth, an abortion. He remained rather offhand about this, showing only a measure of concern for her and none for the child that might have been his.[43] In the same letter he admitted that his desire for marriage and children was dwindling. He was nearly thirty-five and seemed resigned to his single state. This marks a considerable departure from the passionate idealism of his younger days. At around the same time, he wrote to his sister Wil, chronicling the changes in his outlook:

'As for myself, I still persist with the most impossible and highly unsuitable love affairs, from which I come away, as a rule, mired in suffering and shame.

And in my opinion I am absolutely right to do this, reasoning to myself that in former years, when I should have been in love, I sank myself far too deeply in religious and socialist matters, and idolised art more than I do now.'

Letter **W1** (574), to Wil, summer or autumn 1887

His singleness remained near the forefront of his mind even in his final month. In July 1890, he wrote to Theo and Theo's wife, Johanna:

'I still like art and life very much, but I no longer have any great faith that I'll ever find myself a wife.'

Letter **646** (896), to Theo & Jo 2/7/1890

---

[43] Letter **462** (572), to Theo summer 1887.

His great alternative to romance ... and his descent into self-harm

In early 1888, van Gogh moved south from Paris to Arles. He divided his needs for intimacy into two categories, sex and companionship. Sex, he found in the brothel. For companionship, he struck up various friendships, notably with the Roulin family, and he also tried to set up a commune of artists in and around the Yellow House, his rented home. He wrote several times to Theo with great enthusiasm about the project. Sadly, the only taker was Paul Gauguin and he and Vincent were not well matched as housemates. Following a disastrous argument, Vincent cut off his ear,[44] before taking it to a woman named 'Rachel' at a nearby brothel. Gauguin left almost immediately after this. Vincent was hospitalised and once again, found himself on his own.

He later returned to apologise to Rachel and reassure himself that she was all right. Rachel was 'unavailable' to see him, just as Kee Vos had been when eight years earlier he had turned up uninvited at her home. I suspect that the staff at the brothel were protecting Rachel and saying whatever was required to ensure he left quietly. He took their words at face value and wrote to Theo:

> 'Yesterday I went to see the girl who I went to when I was out of my mind. They told me that such incidents are hardly remarkable around here. She did suffer, she fainted but then regained her composure. And beyond that, they say she's fine.'
>
> Letter **576** (745), to Theo 3/2/1889

Vincent went on to hurt himself during further episodes, or 'attacks' as he called them. In August 1889, he described to

---

[44] There has been much debate about this act. Did he remove merely his ear-lobe or did he excise the whole outer ear? Bernadette Murphy's extensive research has unearthed new evidence that points convincingly to the latter (*Van Gogh's Ear*, Bernadette Murphy, Vintage, 2017).

Theo how he been picking up filthy things and eating them.[45] His medical notes state that he had drunk turpentine. His doctor, Dr Peyron, ordered him to stop painting for his own safety; this only left him feeling more frustrated. It was during this time he first mentioned copying Delacroix's 'The Good Samaritan'. He suffered a further attack in the December of 1889. This time he swallowed paint. Dr Peyron insisted that for his own safety, he restrict himself to drawing. He was clearly allowed access to paint again by January, as he produced several copies of paintings by Millet, which Theo acclaimed as possibly his finest work.

We might be picturing Vincent at this point as a shadow of his former self. He had described himself as looking 'haggard', or 'wild-eyed', back in July 1888.[46] In contrast to this, when his sister-in-law Johanna met him for the first time in May 1890, she wrote the following:

> 'I had expected a sick man, but here was a sturdy, broad-shouldered man, with a healthy colour, a smile on his face, and a very resolute appearance ... He seems perfectly well; "He looks much stronger than Theo", was my first thought ... He stayed with us three days and was lively and cheerful all the time.'
>
> *Memoir of Vincent van Gogh*, Jo van Gogh-Bonger

Appearances can be deceptive. Earlier that same month when he painted his Good Samaritan, he was, in many ways, a deeply wounded soul, inwardly if not outwardly 'haggard'; his dreams of domestic bliss were broken, his soul was scarred by the wounds of his unhappy love life, his work pattern was punitive, his mental health was unstable and he was living in constant terror of the next attack, which might destroy his ability to paint for ever.[47]

---

[45] Letter **601** (797), to Theo 22/8/89.
[46] Letter **514** (650), to Theo c. 25/7/1888.
[47] Letter **605** (801), to Theo 10/9/1889.

The Robbers

The robbers are the only characters in the Parable of the Good Samaritan for whom equivalents cannot be found in van Gogh's life.[48] Neither do they appear in his picture. We only see the damage they leave behind. There is no trace of the clothes, animal and goods that were stolen with such violence, just a battered and broken body. Van Gogh had few real villains in his own story. Those who hurt him usually did so without ill intent. Occasionally some retaliated to a hurt he had given them. Those with whom he fell in and out of love did not attack him. Kee Vos' family were remarkably kind to him, despite his provocations. His parents, as we shall see in the next chapter, also wounded him but they never set out with this intention. They failed to understand him. They did not embrace his vocations. They wearied of his behaviour. But they never acted with malice. His greatest enemies were arguably his own extremism and his illnesses, but again these hardly correlate with the robbers in Jesus' story.

In the original parable, the robbers appear, attack and are gone without further commentary. There is almost something inevitable about them, as if they are a fact of the road or even of life itself. They are not named. We know nothing about them beyond the facts that they exist, are known to haunt that road, and can strike at any time. Jesus chooses these faceless robbers to embody the sad truth that bad things can happen in life.

[48] The closest match are the handful of Arlesians who raised a petition against him in 1889. We will discuss them in greater detail in Chapter 5.

Some further thoughts arising from
The Wounded Man and the Robbers

A carefully set-up story

Jesus' parable is very carefully constructed. Every detail of its set-up is important and even the slightest change will affect the parable's overall meanings. Consider the US TV series *Breaking Bad*. The main character, Walter White, discovers he has lung cancer. In order to fund his treatment, he sets up a crystal meth lab. This catapults him into a series of hair-raising encounters with the criminal underworld which run for five full seasons, with further spin-offs. The comedian Marcus Brigstocke once cracked a joke about making a UK version in which a British Walter discovers he has cancer; he gets treated for free by the NHS and recovers. This new version of the story only takes one episode and the series is therefore a flop.[49] When one detail is tweaked, the whole narrative is altered.

In the Parable of the Good Samaritan, the term 'half dead' is crucial and cannot be tweaked. From the attack onwards, this man is completely unaware of all the ensuing drama. He knows nothing about the Priest, Levite or Samaritan. The next thing he will see, presumably, is the inside of a guest room in an inn. A dead body is hard enough to ignore, but it would be much more difficult to pass on by were he semi-conscious and groaning. Both the Priest and Levite would be much more culpable if he calls out to them and they do not stop. This detail, his being left

---

[49] Marcus Brigstocke talking to Gyles Brandreth on *I've Never Seen Star Wars* season 6, episode 4, BBC Radio 4.

'half dead', is just one of several points in Jesus' careful set-up, which if altered or ignored will change everything else.

A story of sin and repentance?

When bad things happen in this life, we might be tempted to seek someone to blame. Remember how the disciples came to Jesus with the question, 'Rabbi, who sinned, this man or his parents, that he was born blind?'[50] There is no one simple answer to why people suffer. The blaming game is rarely helpful. Very few disasters can be pinned down to just one sin. St Paul wrote:

> 'For there is no distinction, since all have sinned and fall short of the glory of God;'
>
> Romans 3:21b-22

Removed from his letter to the Romans and therefore taken out of context, this phrase becomes a rather bitter pill. The Good Samaritan (and other parables) has been coerced, not so much to sweeten it but rather to enforce its swallowing.

There is an unfortunate strand in Christian thinking that tries to fit everything onto a matrix of sin, repentance and forgiveness. When taken to its extremities, preaching becomes quite bizarre; the lost must stomach some very bad news about themselves before being allowed the first hint of good news about Jesus. Amos Starkadder is a worthy example from fiction.[51] Each Sunday he preaches at the Church of the Quivering Brethren, in Howling, Sussex, where the worship is conducted with a poker, to put the congregation in mind of hell fire. He starts each sermon quietly but swiftly builds to a deafening bellow that 'all are damned!' It is easy to parody this kind of theology. Sadly it remains remarkably resilient, though rarely surfacing in such graphic terms as in Jonathan Edwards' infamous 1741 sermon. He preached:

[50] John 9:26.
[51] *Cold Comfort Farm*, Stella Gibbons, 1932.

'The God that holds you over the Pit of Hell, much as one holds a Spider, or some loathsome Insect, over the Fire, abhors you, and is dreadfully provoked; his Wrath towards you burns like Fire; he looks upon you as worthy of nothing else, but to be cast into the Fire; ...'

[and so on, and on *ad* considerable *nauseam* ...]

The Parable of the Good Samaritan takes some considerable distorting to squeeze it onto this matrix. Others fare less well. It is important to remember that it was we, not Jesus, who named the parables. Titles such as 'the Lost Coin', 'the Lost Sheep' and 'the Lost Son' betray this bias. Better but less snappy titles might be, 'the Shepherd who cares for every single one of his sheep', 'the Woman who refuses to allow even one coin to stay lost' and 'the Loving Father who waits for both of his sons to come home'. Jesus' emphasis is on the one who seeks, rather than on any sinful fools whose selfishly land themselves in trouble. The two sons are admittedly in error but it is confusing how a sheep or a coin might consciously make the string of bad decisions which holds them culpable for becoming lost. At least with the Good Samaritan, the title (again, not Jesus') has the right focus and we are not left to unpick 'the parable of the Selfish Man who stupidly went and got himself mugged'. Again, the careful set-up is crucial; Jesus does not begin:

'A proud man, ignoring all warnings and confident in his own strength set out from Jerusalem to Jericho ...'

or,

'A wicked man trying to escape justice took the road from Jerusalem to Jericho ...'

or,

'A foolish young man, stole his dad's expensive new horse for a run down the road from Jerusalem to Jericho ...'.

Without such tweaking, we are left with an uncomfortable message: bad things can happen to us in this life through no fault of our own. The wounded man falls into trouble because he lives in a sin-ridden world, not because he makes sinful choices. He is saved without his needing to repent of anything. His rescue is entirely due to the Samaritan's kindness, whose grace defies any formula. He is saved before he has any awareness of his saviour. Attempts to force this and other parables onto that pattern of sin, repentance and forgiveness damage first Jesus' teaching and then the spiritual lives of those in the pews.

Fear and guilt can produce immediate results, but only at a cost. The invitation of love produces lasting results, but maybe more slowly. The end does not justify the means. Full pews do not necessarily denote healthy churches. *How* we come to faith absolutely affects the *kind* of faith we hold. When we are forced in by fear, our faith will not produce the same fruits as when we drawn in by love. We can turn to God in moments of wretched panic but wretched panic will not keep us with God for good and will always require some unpicking. Jesus' parables are never meant to cow us into trembling submission; rather they show us a living safety net. And it is only as we grow in awareness of God's love, that we become able to contemplate how far we might fall.

In this parable, Jesus offers no plan for cleansing the wilderness of robbers. His Samaritan does not leave the inn on a quest to track them down and bring them to justice. Elsewhere, Jesus requires wrongdoers to face their actions. But here any such addition would be an unnecessary branch-line for our train of thought and would distract us from what he wants to say. Here it is enough to know that life can damage us, and not necessarily through any fault of our own. Sadly, in this life, bad things sometimes come our way and leave us wounded.

Love's wounds

Van Gogh's deepest wounds were received in his quest for love, both romantic and familial. This is not to minimise his agonies over the petitioners of Arles, or an art market that failed to appreciate his work. By the time he left Paris in early 1888, he was in a poor state, both physically and mentally (although he attributed this not to love's wounds but rather to hard working and hard drinking).[52] There was already an aching distance between his youthful idealism and latter resignation. His furious indignation at Kee Vos' rejection waned over the course of the 1880s, to a shrugging recognition that love had passed him by. If ever his former passions returned, he experienced no joy. In a letter from Arles in 1889, he fashioned an analogy, explaining such stirrings to Theo:

> 'At times, just as the waves break against the stone-deaf, stone-hearted cliffs, along comes a storm of desire to kiss something, a farmyard hen type of woman, but then I have to take this for what it is, the product of hysterical overexcitement rather than any proper vision of reality.'
>
> Letter **587** (763), to Theo 22-28/4/1889

There is such sadness in this. He did not share Miss Havisham's bitterness;[53] rather, he appears simply exhausted. He saw himself as a rock face: hopeless, sullen and stony. Love's waves brought no delight, they only battered him, distressing and further eroding him whilst reminding him of all that had eluded him. He wearily accepted a future where love was no longer an option.

[52] Letter **553a** (695) to Paul Gauguin 3/10/1888.

[53] Charles Dickens' character in *Great Expectations* was jilted at the altar and insisted on wearing her wedding dress every day for the rest of her life.

Love can come later in life but after a few knock-backs it is never quite as dizzying as our youthful escapades. Van Gogh read and reread Hugo's *Les Misérables*. In this novel he encountered not just the happy whirlwind of Cosette and Marius, but also the tragedies of Éponine and Fantine, who stand as stark warnings that the wounds of love, especially those of blind devotion, can be fatal. The wounds of love can drive us into permanent retreat or they can make us wiser. It is always a tragedy if ever we are wounded so deeply that we can never countenance dancing to love's tune again. In the aftermath of Kee's rejection, Vincent told Theo:

'A person can get over it once, if he is foiled and wounded in love and in his affairs and plans. But that must not happen too often.'

Letter **216** (247), to Theo 19/7/1882

It seems for him that he was 'wounded in love' too many times. We might seek a life without any such trauma. We could try living without love altogether. We would need to forget van Gogh's analogy about the sails on the little ship. Remember how adamant he was that 'life without love' was impossible. In the following century, C. S. Lewis would write even more starkly about the folly of trying to avoid love's pain:

'There is no safe investment. To love at all is to be vulnerable. Love anything, and your heart will certainly be wrung and possibly be broken. If you want to make sure of keeping it intact, you must give your heart to no one, not even an animal … The only place outside Heaven where you can be perfectly safe from all the dangers and perturbations of love is Hell.'[54]

[54] *The Four Loves* by C. S. Lewis © copyright C. S. Lewis Pte Ltd 1960. Used with the kind permission of the C. S. Lewis Company Ltd.

The Wounded Man and the Robbers

Love's wounds find no cure when we shun love. Love's wounds can be healed only by love. The next person to arrive on the scene is a priest, and as such should be well versed in these matters.

CHAPTER 4

The Priest

'Now by chance a priest was going down that road;
and when he saw him, he passed by on the other side.'

Luke 10:31

Van Gogh's painting

The Priest *is* there in van Gogh's painting, but you might miss him. He is far from obvious. Follow the winding road, up through the mid-ground, and you will find him. He is just about to vanish from sight, either around a corner or downwards, if the road descends into a new gully.

Whilst he might not be immediately obvious to the casual observer, there is no such thing as a casual traveller on this road. Both the Levite and the Samaritan would know that he has recently passed this way.

The Priest is painted with just a few downward flowing brushstrokes, similar to those used for the vertical gorge walls ahead of him. His colours are almost identical too; he has been given their muted browns and bluish greens. Were it not for a ray of sunlight catching his turban and left-hand side, he might disappear altogether, becoming indistinguishable from the rock face. Is this akin to that wish of many conflicted people – seeking to fade into the background until an awkward moment has passed by? The Priest almost achieves this. Give him another minute and he will be out of shot and away.

One quibble with van Gogh, and by extension with Delacroix, is that this Priest makes his journey on foot. If the Samaritan comes riding an animal then both the Priest and the Levite are likely to do the same. This was a dangerous road, entirely unsuitable for lone pedestrians. We can assume that when the robber stole the wounded man's clothes, they also stole his horse, mule or donkey. The Samaritan clearly rides along the road. His animal is explicit in both parable and painting. If he alone has a beast of burden then he has a significant advantage over both Priest and Levite. They might defend their neglect thus: *'Well what was I supposed to do? Just sit with him? Wait for the next passer-by and hope it's not another robber? Surely you must see, he was far too heavy for me to carry by myself? Naturally, if I'd had a horse … or even a donkey, well of course I'd have stopped …'* Jesus' parable works best when there is a level playing field and the Priest, Levite and Samaritan all appear at the scene, equally equipped to help the wounded man.

Van Gogh's 'priests'

Theodorus van Gogh
To whom did Vincent's thoughts turn as he painted this figure? The most likely candidate was the religious minister best known to him: his own father, Theodorus van Gogh. He was a pastor, who served in various rural parishes throughout Vincent's life.

The two of them had an unsettled relationship, to say the least. His father offered four main targets for Vincent's frustrations. He was a clergyman and, as such, embodied the religious world that his son embraced all too zealously before discarding utterly. He was always on the disapproving side of Vincent's romantic choices. He was unable to engage well with his sons' artistic world. Vincent was emphatic: 'Pa is not the man to get mixed up in artistic matters.'[55] He had a fundamentally different temperament; Theodorus was a quiet, conservative-minded man whereas Vincent was both wilful and passionate. Jo van Gogh-Bonger wrote, presumably having listened to Vincent's mother:

> 'As a child he [Vincent] was of a difficult temper, often troublesome and self-willed; his upbringing was not fitted to counterbalance these faults, as his parents were very tender-hearted, especially towards their eldest.'
>
> *Memoir of Vincent van Gogh,* Johanna van Gogh-Bonger

Vincent's filial devotion changes rapidly in his twenties, from being overly adoring to angrily critical of his father. Compare the following two excerpts from his letters to Theo. The first is from when Vincent was twenty-three:

> 'It is my prayer and deepest desire, that the spirit of my Father and Grandfather also might rest upon me, and that it might be granted to me to be a Christian and a Christian labourer, that my life might resemble, the more the better, theirs whom I have just mentioned; you see, the old wine is good and I do not desire the new. Their God will be my God and their people will be my people, that this may be my portion: to come to know Christ in His full worth and to be compelled by His love.'
>
> Letter **89** (109), to Theo 22/3/1877

---

[55] Letter **164** (193), to Theo 21/12/1881.

He wrote the second just short of five years later:

> 'Pa is not the type of person for whom I can feel what I feel
> for example, for you or for Mauve. I genuinely love Pa and
> Ma but it is a completely different feeling from the kind I
> have for you and for M. Pa cannot sympathise or empathise
> with me and I cannot accommodate myself within Pa and
> Ma's strictures, which are so cramped, they would suffocate
> me.'
>
> Letter **164** (193), to Theo 21/12/1881

Their relationship continued, bumping along, in and out of
this same rut until Theodorus's death in 1885. The frustration
was not felt solely by Vincent; Theodorus seriously considered
having him sectioned for his mental health, or, put in the terms
of the 1880s, committed to the lunatic asylum in Gheel. He
described his eldest with both pity and irritation:

> 'It grieves us so to see that he [Vincent] literally knows no
> joy of life, but always walks with bent head, whilst we did
> all in our power to bring him to an honourable position! It
> seems as if he deliberately chooses the most difficult path.'
>
> *Memoir of Vincent van Gogh,* Johanna van Gogh-Bonger

Vincent's complaints were many. Along with the 'Jesuitisms', he
hated the way his father did not listen to him. He complained
that his views went 'in one ear and out of the other' whilst his
father could say such devastating things as, 'You're killing me',
while reading the newspaper and calmly smoking his pipe.[56]
At other times Theodorus could erupt with ferocious anger,
expecting Vincent to cower and give way; this was something he
had learnt not to do by the age of twenty-eight. He complained
to Theo:

---

[56] Letter **169** (199), to Theo 7 or 8/1/1882.

'Pa is terribly sensitive and irritable and full of whims in domestic matters and used to getting his own way. And under the heading "the rules and regulations of this house" to which I am obliged to conform, literally everything marches to the tune of Pa's whims.'

Letter 169 (199), to Theo 7 or 8/1/1882

Vincent found himself, on more than one occasion, living as an adult in his parents' home. These times were clearly difficult for all involved. Vincent set out his side of the awkward situation at length, likening himself not to a bull in a china shop, but to a large shaggy sheepdog in a respectable household. What follows is my paraphrase, in which I seek to capture the essence of his analogy without domesticating it. He wrote this privately to Theo with no thought of being quoted more than a century later. As such, it leaps and bounds across two letters, full of wit and angry passion:[57]

'Father and Mother shrink from taking me in as if I were a large shaggy sheepdog.

They feel obliged to be kind, yet remain on edge – ever fearful of this dog getting in everyone's way:

"What mess will his wet paws make in our well-ordered rooms? And surely his loud bark will alarm our other, more refined guests. And we often have clergymen visiting, whatever will they think? And he's so very shaggy – positively filthy! And what if he bit someone? Or went mad? Well, maybe the village policeman would shoot him."

The shaggy sheepdog takes all of this in. He knows the household is too genteel for him, that his presence is more tolerated than welcomed. He suggests a way forward ...

---

[57] See Appendix for a translation of the full, original version.

Could he be like a guard dog? But, "No thank you", they say. "It's peaceful and perfectly safe here, there's no trouble." And so he shuts up.

The shaggy sheepdog is able to think like this because once, long ago, before he was a shaggy sheepdog, he was a human and a son of this household. They remember this whilst forgetting that he only became so shaggy and so unkempt, because they left him out in the streets once too often.

The shaggy sheepdog considers his return a weakness and vows not to repeat his mistake. He chooses instead to remain as he is; a poor dog with a fine tuned human nature. And he dreams of finding a kennel of his own or even returning to the wild heath, where though alone, he was never as lonely, as he is now.[58]

The bad feelings between father and eldest son often spilt over into Vincent's relationship with Theo. Theo for his part, found himself caught in the middle. On occasion he took Vincent to task, and Vincent in turn became so enraged that he accused Theo of being 'Father II', insisting that 'Father I' was more than enough.[59] At other times Theo calmed their parents' anger, paving the way for yet another reconciliation.[60]

There are several stories of Theodorus's kindnesses; Vincent tells some of these himself. His father tried to find work for him. He visited him in the Borinage, when his extremism was causing alarm. He reasoned with him, persuading him to take a step back from his self-imposed poverty and return to his given

[58] Paraphrase from Letter **346** (413), to Theo 15/12/1883 & Letter **347** (414), to Theo 17/12/1883.
[59] Letter **358** to Theo 1/3/1884 (although the Van Gogh Museum includes this quotation in Letter **474**, to Theo 10/12/1884.
[60] Letter **227** (258), to Theo 20/8/1882.

lodgings.[61] He sometimes bought his son new clothes. He and Vincent's mother sent him a parcel shortly after Sien's baby was born (Vincent himself was newly discharged from hospital, having been treated for gonorrhoea). This parcel contained a coat, tobacco, cigars, a cake and underwear. Vincent took this as a hopeful sign of their acceptance of his new life.[62] A later package contained a warm winter coat for Sien.[63] Vincent was still grateful eight months later and declared to Theo that, in exchange for this one kind deed, he would put up with a whole mudslide of words about him.[64] His father took him in again after his relationship with Sien had ended and helped him to create a studio in the parsonage's mangle room. His final written words about Vincent were, 'May he meet with success anyhow.'[65]

With hindsight, Vincent claimed he respected his parents' relationship, going so far as to say that as a married couple they were 'exemplary'.[66] He often claimed to love his father, although he usually followed this with a 'but' and a complaint about his being misunderstood.

Other 'priests' and clergy

Theodorus van Gogh was not the only member of the clergy in the family. Vincent's uncle, the Reverend Johannes Stricker, was also ordained. He was the father of Kee Vos, the woman Vincent loved so obsessively. As discussed in the previous chapter, Vincent refused to accept Kee's rejection of him and her parents were required to intervene. Despite their kindness, Vincent was badly hurt by the whole incident and ever after this wound was inextricably interwoven in his mind with 'the clergy'. His own parents had also sought to calm his suit. Thus,

---

[61] *Memoir of Vincent van Gogh*, Jo van Gogh-Bonger, December 1913.
[62] Letter **220** (251), to Theo 26/7/1882.
[63] Letter **236** (271), to Theo 8/10/1882.
[64] Letter **291** (351), to Theo 5 or 6/6/1883.
[65] *Memoir of Vincent van Gogh*, Jo van Gogh-Bonger, December 1913.
[66] Letter **573** (741), to Theo 23/1/1889.

from his perspective, they forbade him first the respectable Kee and soon afterwards the disrespectable Sien, only reinforcing his conviction that clerics despised love. He wrote to Theo:

> 'The clergy call us sinners, conceived in sin and born in sin. Bah! What utter nonsense! Is it sinful to love, to need love, to be unable to live without love? I think a life without love is both sinful and immoral.'
>
> Letter **164** (193), to Theo 21/12/1881

During the winter of 1881–2, Vincent lost not only his respect for the clergy but for all organised religion. It is hard to believe that none of this painful history passed through his mind in the Spring of 1890, as he considered Delacroix's lithograph and then made those few muted brushstrokes that depict the Priest in his own version of the Good Samaritan.

His anti-clerical views can only have been reinforced in the summer of 1885, when the Catholic clergy in Neunen warned people to stop posing for him. His father had only just died when these priests picked up the baton of clerical cluelessness, at least in Vincent's eyes. They believed, wrongly, that he had got a local girl pregnant and was therefore a threat to their parishioners' morality. This angered Vincent on two counts; first there was the unfair, unfounded accusation, and then came their condescending manner – they warned him of the dangers of mixing with the 'lower orders' but then took a much more threatening tone when upbraiding his prospective models. To Vincent they thus appeared snobbish, ridiculous, loveless and bullying.

There was another clergyman who played a significant role in Vincent's life. The Reverend Mr Salles was a protestant minister in the south of France. He met the ailing Dutchman in Arles and befriended him. He showed him much kindness and, when the time came, helped him to move to the asylum at Saint-Rémy. He also corresponded with Theo, ensuring he was up to date with all of Vincent's latest news. If Vincent thought at all about Mr Salles as he worked, I hope that it was as he painted the Samaritan, rather than the Priest.

The Priest in Jesus' parable

Leaving aside for a moment Theodorus van Gogh and other Dutch clergy, we return to the original parable. Jesus deliberately chooses a priest to be the first to arrive at the scene of the crime. Perhaps we need a line or two about priests at the time of Jesus, to banish thoughts of dog-collars and any other confusions arising from various faiths using the same word to describe different offices.

The priesthood Jesus knew was inherited; if your father was a priest, then you too would be a priest. This dated back all the way to Aaron, Moses' brother. Priests lived by stricter codes than their fellow Jews. Certain aspects of the Law were written expressly for them, forbidding them from some activities, thus freeing them to carry out their duties. There were different types of priests; some were simply 'priests' and others 'high priests', sometimes called 'chief priests'. John the Baptist's father, Zechariah, is the first priest we meet in Luke's Gospel. He, like our Priest in the parable, was an ordinary priest. We see in his story an example of the kind of Temple services performed by the priests. There was a duty rota shared between different groups of priests. We meet Zechariah when he was singled out from his group, to enter the sanctuary and offer incense while, outside, his colleagues prayed.

We do not know why the Priest in the parable was travelling on the road. We might guess that he has some sort of ritual to perform in Jericho. We are not told if he is rich or poor, if he is deeply committed to the establishment or a bit of a rebel. All that Jesus says is that he, a Priest, sees the wounded man and then passes by on the other side.

Why does this Priest not stop? Perhaps van Gogh would deem him just as 'clueless' about love as certain clergy he had encountered. There are several more theories, some of which are alarmingly quick to stereotype Jewish Priests as self-interested and Judaism as overly concerned with its rituals. These arouse suspicions of an unpleasant bias lurking behind some of the scholarship. Over the centuries, academic Christianity has at times fuelled antisemitism, both consciously and unwittingly.

In truth, we will never have definitive reasons for an individual character's every motivation in a story. However, we do know that even though he should stop, he does not. The Scriptures instruct him:

'... you shall love your neighbour as yourself: I am the Lord.'
Leviticus 19:18

And even if the Priest is the kind of man who thinks, *'But this man might not be my neighbour and if he's not Jewish then I have no duty to him. And how can I tell if he's Jewish or not when he's been stripped of the very clothes that would identify him as Jewish?'*, the same chapter in Leviticus makes it clear that his duty to care applies to all people:

'The alien who resides with you shall be to you as the citizen among you; you shall love the alien as yourself, for you were aliens in the land of Egypt: I am the Lord your God.'
Leviticus 19:34

And what if the wounded man is no longer half dead? What if he is now actually dead? Again, according to some sources this priest's role is clear. Both Philo and Josephus, himself a priest, are unequivocal about this. The Talmud is equally forthright.[67] He must bury him.

[67] see *Short Stories by Jesus*, Amy-Jill Levine, HarperOne 2015. On page 101 she quotes the following sources to back this point: Philo 'Hypothetica', Josephus 'Against Appion' The Mishnah, The Babylonian Talmud, Nazir and the Jerusalem Talmud.

The Priest is surely aware of the Talmud and the kind of thinking that Josephus and Philo later committed to paper. But suppose he was thinking about other passages in Leviticus? One says:

> 'No one shall defile himself for a dead person among his relatives, except for his nearest kin: his mother, his father, his son, his daughter, his brother.'
>
> Leviticus 21:1-3

Also, he might have dug up a memory of some other Talmudic verses, insisting on a clear four cubits between a priest and a corpse. If he does have priestly duties in Jericho, he might resent the inconvenience of a return to Jerusalem, to renew his cleanliness. Perhaps a stray thought pops into his head, sounding, at a push, like it might be from the Torah. Ben Sirach counselled:

> 'Give to the devout, but do not help the sinner.
>
> Do good to the humble, but do not give to the ungodly; hold back their bread, and do not give it to them.'
>
> The Wisdom of Ben Sirach 12:4-5a

This, however, is not part of the Torah, just as, 'God helps those who help themselves,' is not part of the Christian Bible, even though it is frequently quoted as if it is. Possibly this or some other scripturally-sounding verse comes to him in that split-second as he makes his decision. But either way, if this wounded figure is dead or if he is alive, this Priest should not simply pass him by; even if he has fears about becoming defiled, he still has duties to perform.

All this might be unnecessarily complicated. Maybe he is simply frightened that the robbers are still around and his decision to move on almost makes itself. Maybe he is conflicted but keeps on walking until the time for decision-making has passed. When faced with a difficult decision, we as humans will often scout around for the simplest way ahead. If we are religious, we might seek scriptural verses, either to guide us or to justify our initial reactions. The problem is that the ancient Scriptures rarely speak with one clear voice, having been written by different people over several centuries, and are then interpreted and re-interpreted as time progresses. For any one subject, there could be several passages and key-verses contending to offer guidance. The question becomes one of priorities. We do well if we ask less about being 'faithful to the Scriptures' but rather seek to be faithful to God, as we understand God from the whole of Scripture. And, within this process, we should never underestimate our propensity to delude ourselves.

There are good reasons for the Priest to stop. There could be any number of reasons, not quite as good, but also not plain evil, why he should not stop. Remember that he too is alone. If we attempted to tweak the story so that it said, *'now by chance two priests were going down that road …'*, or, better still, *'a group of priests …'*, it would become a very different matter. But Jesus sets up a tightly-designed story about extreme circumstances. He has his own intentions for this parable and these deliberately do not allow wiggle room for such red herrings as, *'How many priests does it take to help a wounded man?'*

If we must judge, then we do well not to judge too harshly. Better still, we might reflect on some of the split-second decisions we have made when self-preservation was jostling with some other good cause. If we found ourselves cast as the Priest in a film version of this story, we should understand the weight of his decision and, like good actors, allow a number of complex emotions to trace their paths across our faces. Or, perhaps, he gives as much time to all these competing options and verses, as to a blink of his eye. He might drive all awkward thoughts from his mind, so that his decision barely registers in his short-term memory and finds no purchase in the long-term.

In short, by the time he has reached the distant blue grey corner of van Gogh's painting, the Priest might have forgotten there ever was a wounded man by the roadside. We are left guessing. We only know for sure that he sees him and passes by on the other side.

Some further thoughts arising from
The Priest

Religion without love

Vincent van Gogh concluded that the organised religion of his day took too narrow a view of love. His experience was limited to Christianity in its Protestant and Roman Catholic forms, but there is nothing to suggest that any other organised religion might have had a greater appeal for him. He believed that Christian clergy wrote him off as an 'unbeliever' because his life did not tick enough of their prescribed boxes. If they did so, that was unfair. He explained to Theo that he still believed, albeit without the blinkers of his previous devotion, and in ways that defied conventional categorisations:

> 'You see, I find the God of the clergy as dead as a doornail. But does that make me an atheist? The clergy regard me thus – que soit[68] – but look, I love and how could I feel love were I myself not alive or were others not alive? And if we are alive, there is something wondrous in it. Call it what you will, God or human nature but there is certainly something that I cannot define using a set system, although it is definitely alive and real, and see, that for me is God or as good as God.'
>
> Letter **164** (193), to Theo 21/12/81

He wrote this in the midst of his agonies over Kee's rejection. A month prior to this, he argued:

[68] Van Gogh wrote this letter in Dutch, apart from the phrase, 'que soit' (the French for 'whatever').

'Also it occurs to me the word 'God' would sound insincere if love had to be buried away and one wasn't allowed to follow the voice of one's heart.'

Letter **158** (185) to Theo 18/11/81

God-talk can be an insincere noise whenever churches value reputation and respectability above all else. Shaggy sheepdogs get the message soon enough from holy huddles and sanctimonious self-interest groups; for all the talk of love, they know they are not welcome. In contrast, healthy churches will have a motley collection of lost souls, who might bound around leaving metaphorical muddy paw prints everywhere, but no one minds too much, because God's welcome is always uppermost.

Some people argue, as I have in the past, that the Priest in the parable might be personally less culpable than his institution for this lack of practical love on the roadside. My mind is changing. If the current culture of his workplace, the Temple, really is so rule-bound as to legitimise such lovelessness, then he has two duties:

1. To campaign for change, loudly and persistently protesting against any such love-denying ordinances within his institution,

and then,

2. he *still* has a duty to stop on the road, either to help or to bury this human, according to his needs.

Both of these duties are easier to name than to perform, especially if the Priest is alone and unsupported. Added to this, ailing or corrupt institutions often discourage protest and train their aspiring leaders to keep quiet.[69]

---

[69] This point is eloquently made by Rosie Harper, in her chapter 'What's under the bonnet?' pages 74-77, in *Letters to a Broken Church*, edited by Janet Fife and Gilo, Ekklesia, 2019.

The Priest

Like van Gogh, Jesus clearly had several gripes with the religious establishment of his day. He could populate his story with a butcher and a baker. Instead, he chooses religious characters – a Priest and a Levite. We can see this as Jesus campaigning for change and making his own protest about the way the Temple is being run. He more than implies that its current representatives are of no use to those who are hard to rescue. He then adds this small detail about the Samaritan pouring out wine and oil onto the wounds of the stranger. During services, the priests would pour out wine and oil as offerings. Is Jesus then suggesting that such specifically religious acts are more meaningful in the gutter than in the Temple? And that this good worship can be offered by anyone, even the unqualified – even a Samaritan? I imagine a variety of reactions from Jesus' first audiences; any priests or Levites present could well feel that he was 'having a pop', not just at them or their office but at their entire institution.

Life without love

Vincent van Gogh had no respect for religion or art that was without love. We should probably add music to that list. He wrote with great enthusiasm about Wagner and Berlioz. I have a hunch that if music had been as readily available then as now, he would have written much more about it. His letters to Theo would be filled with recommendations for streaming this band, listening to that performer, and tracking down that one rare recording that outshines all the others. In January 1889, he told Gauguin that the music of Wagner and Berlioz was 'an art that consoles the broken-hearted!'[70] The two artists shared a love for the kind of music that is not simply heard, but also felt. And his ambition was to paint in the same way. At this point he could have strayed into scripture and quoted St Paul, who maintained that nothing was gained from any number of extreme achievements, if they were done without love:

[70] Letter **572a** (739), to Gauguin c. 22/1/1889,

'If I speak in the tongues of mortals and of angels, but do not have love, I am a noisy gong or a clanging cymbal.'

1 Corinthians 13:1

If there is a God, and if that God is the same God for whom Jesus of Nazareth lived, then that God is love. Any construct on any foundation other than this love is doomed to end. The temptation might be to turn 'God is love' around to 'love is God'. Love, however, comes from God. The 'is' is not an 'equals' and does not permit such reversals. If we deify love, we set ourselves on a road that ultimately leads away from love. For Jesus, love is never separated from God or turned around to replace God. His parable of the Good Samaritan offers inspiration for a new society built on God's love, since God's love requires us to recognise our human neighbour in every wounded figure. The parable is far richer than any simple summation along the lines of *'… and therefore we must love everyone.'* As we shall see in subsequent chapters, this many-layered story certainly *is* about human love, *and* is also the story of God's love. This is the love that is kinder than our religious institutions and far deeper than the resources of their human representatives, be they clergy, priest or as we shall now see, Levite.

CHAPTER 5

The Levite

'So likewise a Levite, when he came to the place
   and saw him,
passed by on the other side.'

Luke 10:32

Van Gogh's painting

The Levite is a better-defined figure than the Priest. He is closer
to us. Not that that matters; we are still lost to him. His back is
outlined by dark brush strokes, thicker than at his front, as if van
Gogh was re-stating his decision to press on and get away from
all that is now behind him. None of his defining lines, however,
even those at his back, are as bold as those van Gogh gave to the
Samaritan or to the wounded man. It is they, not the Levite,

who are the focus. The Samaritan occupies a place that could have been the Levite's, had he not chosen his lesser role.

Apart from his costly purple hat, he is dressed in the same muted hues as the Priest. He appears just a hint brighter, as he has yet to lose himself in the mist. The Priest seems free to pursue the open road; at his distance, there is only open blue space before him. The Levite however is surrounded by van Gogh's swirling strokes of the grey-green and yellow undergrowth by the roadside. He interrupts their flow as they swoop over his shoulder, turning back on him, almost as if aiming for his chest and urging him to reconsider. He still could. Unlike the Priest, he has yet to pass that point beyond which he cannot reasonably return. The wounded man is still just behind him.

However, his shoulders are hunched as if against the cold, but more likely in the determined effort to ignore any instinct to turn back. His head is bowed forward, suggesting his eyes are locked in concentration on the path before him. Perhaps he hopes that what he cannot see will cease to exist. Perhaps he is wishing he had been this focused on the path a moment beforehand; then he might not have seen the wounded man and thus been spared the awkward decision, to stop or pass on by.

His arms seem slightly foreshortened, and his hands are out of sight; they are probably not stuffed into his pockets, but rather clasped together over his chest, with their knuckles resolutely pointing forward.

He does not run, yet he walks with purposeful deliberation. His feet are hidden from us. Our line of sight is blocked by the Samaritan's travelling chest, wildly thrown open and then tossed aside. This abandon contrasts utterly with the Levite's measured pace, and his tightly guarded bodily chest containing his heart and his resources, which remain firmly closed to the man in need.

Who is this Levite? Again, as with the Priest, we know nothing about him personally, but we do know some of his tasks. Levites, like priests, are the descendants of Levi, the son of Jacob. They are a much larger group which includes the priests.

At the time of the parable, they sang psalms during services, they were involved in Temple maintenance, and at other times they served as stewards or guards.

Why does the Levite not stop? Again, Jesus does not give us a list of his possible motives. The Levite within the parable has the same duties as the Priest, to help or to bury the man. He shares the same risk of being attacked but the Priest has already passed on by, and, following this lead, the Levite might reassure himself, *'Well if a priest saw reason to get away from here, that'll do for me too.'* If this is so, his fears win the day conclusively. All he needs to do now is move on quickly and forget all about the man, who is *'Surely beyond any help I could give ... and, very possibly, in fact very probably dead anyway.'*

Van Gogh's 'Levites'

We can ponder who might have visited Vincent van Gogh's mind as he painted the figure of this Levite. There are several people who did not give him the help he wanted for his journey. None of these make perfect matches for the Levite, but some come closer than others.

Mr H. G. Tersteeg (H. G. T.)

Mr H. G. Tersteeg was Vincent's boss at Goupil & Cie. He was an artist in his own right, as well as a successful art dealer and business man. Initially, the two got on very well. Vincent went so far as to fill a small book with sketches for as a gift for Mr Tersteeg's small daughter, Betsy.[71] Their relationship continued despite Vincent's dismissal from the firm, with Mr Tersteeg advancing him money at times, when Theo's letters were late.[72] Vincent sent him drawings and eagerly awaited his comments, convinced that Mr Tersteeg's approval would boost his career.[73]

---

[71] This sketchbook is now in the van Gogh museum in Amsterdam.

[72] Letter **169** (198), to Theo 7 or 8/1/1882.

[73] Letter **152** (175), to Theo 12 to 15/10/1881.

In time, it became clear that Mr Tersteeg did not 'get' Vincent as an artist. He did not appreciate how much time Vincent wanted to spend in training, admittedly not in any formal academy but rather as an autodidact, out with his sketchbook and learning the craft of drawing with models of his own choosing. Mr Tersteeg, as his mentor, might have had a point. Who can tell what turns Vincent's career might have taken, had he accepted a more conventional approach in these early days? As it was, Vincent spent several years writing to Theo, speculating about some vague, but ever-receding future date when he would start producing work that would be saleable.

It was not just this unorthodox approach to training that bothered Mr Tersteeg. He disapproved of Vincent's style, claiming that he was incapable of decent watercolours. Vincent was not a compliant mentee and countered that he would only ever produce work that bore the stamp of his own character.[74]

In Mr Tersteeg's mind, there was a large question mark over Vincent's character; Vincent complained to Theo that he viewed him as a 'duffer and dreamer'.[75] This was just as their relationship was beginning to sour; Mr Tersteeg did not approve of Sien at all. The day came when he turned up at Vincent's studio in 'a policeman-like mood'.[76] He expressed his strongest feelings about an aspiring artist consorting with a prostitute and her children. He said as much in Sien's presence, the cold force of his words making her wither. This kind of opposition was guaranteed to strengthen Vincent's resolve about the rightness of his path, and to dig his heels in further against the hypocrisy of the older generation, whether they be clergy or not. He declared that should Mr Tersteeg continue in this manner, he would have nothing more to do with him ever again. Later, in the same letter, he predicted to Theo that Mr Tersteeg would

---

[74] Letter **180** (210), to Theo 11/3/1882.
[75] Letter **180** (210), to Theo 11/3/1882.
[76] Letter **216** (247), to Theo 18/7/1882.

stand back and watch Sien drown without lifting a finger to save her, deeming her death a good thing for society. To Vincent in 1882, Mr Tersteeg stood accused of a callous neglect, far worse than that of either Priest or Levite.

In later years, long after he and Sien had parted, Vincent rediscovered his respect for his former mentor. He encouraged Theo to form a working partnership with him, arguing that their combined powers would certainly attract investors.[77] Mr Tersteeg's good opinion remained tantalisingly attractive to him. He predicted that if Mr Tersteeg viewed Sisley as working like a drunkard, he would surely reject Vincent as one in the grip of 'a raging case of delirium tremens'. But then again, he might just catch the extraordinary potential in 'The Night Café' ... Vincent considered the risk worth taking.[78]

Anton Mauve

Anton Mauve was an established artist and also a relative, by marriage. In 1881 Vincent spent three weeks in his studio, where Mauve encouraged him to experiment with oil and watercolour. Up to this point Vincent had concentrated on drawing. It is near on impossible for us to imagine him not using colour. Maybe he would have come to it by himself. As it was, Mauve deserves some credit, for planting a seed that later would bear such astonishing fruit.

Vincent deeply respected Mauve as an artist, as an intellectual and as a wit, enjoying those occasions when Mauve mimicked preachers. He relied on Mauve's judgements. When hunting for a studio he told Theo that he would make no firm decision without first consulting Mauve,[79] who went on to loan him some money once he had found a place at 138 Schenkweg in The Hague. He rapidly became, in Vincent's mind, a new father figure, in every way wiser than old Theodorus back at home.

---

[77] Letter **468** (584), to Theo 10/3/1888.
[78] Letter **534** (677), to Theo 9/9/1888.
[79] Letter **164** (193), to Theo 21/12/1881.

They sometimes annoyed each other, but not in any serious way, at least not until Sien had arrived. Mauve then joined Tersteeg and Vincent's parents in disapproving of her. Vincent consequently banished Mauve from his life:

> 'Dear Theo,
> Today I met Mauve and had a highly regrettable conversation with him, and it has become clear to me that Mauve and I have parted ways permanently. Mauve has gone too far to retract, at least he certainly would not want to. I invited him to come and see my work and then talk things over. Mauve refused unreservedly, "I certainly will not come to see you, those days are over."
>
> He finished with, "You have a vicious character." At this point I turned away – this was in the dunes – and walked home by myself.'
>
> Letter **192** (224), to Theo 3-12/5/1882

There is always more than one side to a story. We can only guess at what led Mauve to resort to the cruel words 'a vicious character'. Following this he became yet another person who stopped for a while but then passed on by, leaving Vincent on his increasingly lonely road.

However, as with Tersteeg, Vincent later forgot his grudges. He had never lost his respect for Mauve as an artist and was clearly upset in 1888, when the news of his death reached him in Arles. Vincent immediately painted an orchard in blossom and sent it to Mauve's widow in the Netherlands, as a gift in memoriam.

Paul Gauguin

I wondered for quite some time whether or not Paul Gauguin had a place in this chapter. From one stance, he seems a good match for the Levite; a man suffers such a bad breakdown that he cuts off his own ear, immediately following which his housemate scarpers off back to Paris. This would make a 'neat fit', but it would not be fair to Gauguin. It ignores too many facts. Gauguin moved to Arles, not as Vincent's friend but as a fellow professional artist, with the sole purpose of advancing his career. He was not a mental health nurse, neither was his disposition that of a natural carer. He found himself living, in midwinter, in a small house with a man whose mental state was plummeting. The two of them barely knew each other before they started sharing living space, working space and meals. The whole project was born of Vincent's fantasy of creating a brotherhood of artists in Provence. It is hard to imagine how it could ever have worked, especially given this combination of characters.

Gauguin did not 'pass by on the other side', abandoning a dying Vincent. He contacted Theo by telegram and possibly met him from the Paris train on Christmas Day. He certainly escorted him to the hospital,[80] but did not visit Vincent himself, fearing his presence might cause him further trauma. The two of them maintained a regular correspondence until the end of Vincent's life. His actions, by no means comparable with the generosity of the Good Samaritan, are also not as neglectful as those of the Levite.

My project, however, is less about a fair hearing for Gauguin and more about Vincent's memories as he painted his Good Samaritan. There is a clue that points to Vincent finding some kind of Levite-like quality in Gauguin. He wrote to Theo in January 1889, less than a month after his breakdown, with a reference to a novel in which the main character, Tartarin, abandons a friend in the Alps:

'And you, since you wish to know how things were, have you ever read the whole of Tartarin. – That would teach you fairly well how to recognise Gauguin. With all seriousness, I encourage you to reread this passage in Daudet's book.'

Letter **571** (736), to Theo, 17/1/1889

---

[80] Bernadette Murphy has identified in one of Gauguin's sketches, a fountain in the hospital grounds (*Van Gogh's Ear*, Vintage 2016, page 134).

A few days later he wrote to 'Mon cher ami Gauguin', saying he was troubled by his friend's departure, reproaching himself as the possible cause. But at the end of this letter he slipped in a seemingly innocent question about reading the whole of Tartarin's story, accompanied by a cryptic statement about friendships formed in the South.[81]

Fairly or unfairly, Gauguin might well have appeared in Vincent's mind as he painted the Levite, but perhaps more for abandoning his great Provencal project than for deserting him in his hour of need. Vincent kept up their correspondence and never ceased pondering the reasons for his departure whilst hoping they might work together again.[82] They never did.

The 'eighty' petitioners of Arles

One of the bitterest moments in all of Vincent's life came in the February of 1889. He was due to be discharged from the hospital in Arles. He had been there on and off since the end of December, following the incident in which he had cut off his ear. Some of the townsfolk raised a petition, asking the Mayor to keep him confined for a further month, nominally in fear of his dangerous behaviour. Vincent believed that they had collected eighty signatures.[83] In emotional terms, the damage was immense. He wrote to Theo:

'So you can understand what a stunning blow it was, straight to my heart, as I discovered just how many people were so cowardly that they'd gang up on one lone man – and him an ill man.'

Letter **579** (750), to Theo 19/3/1889

[81] Letter **572a** (739) to Paul Gauguin, 21/1/1889 .
[82] Letter **605** (801) to Theo 10/9/1889, Letter **610** (810) to Theo 8/10/1889, Letter **620** (833) to Theo 1/1/1890.
[83] Letter **579** (750), to Theo 19/3/1889.

Recent research reveals the true number was only thirty, four of whom were illiterate and yet managed to sign anyway. In rational terms, this means that a small group of people got into a lather for long enough to persuade some others to sign a piece of paper.[84] The most obvious instigator is a Monsieur Soulé, Vincent's landlord. He has a clear motive for keeping Vincent away from Arles; he had signed over the lease of the Yellow House to a tobacconist, never imagining that Vincent would return from hospital. Most likely the petition was lodged in the grocer's shop next door to the Yellow House, as the proprietor, Monsieur Crévoulin, was the first to sign. He was fed up with the gawkers who had taken to hanging around the square, hoping for a sight of the man with one ear. Once the petition was underway a small furore gained momentum and ever-more serious reports of Vincent's behaviour were filed with the police. Its starting point however, was less the fear of Vincent's madness and more Soulé's and Crévoulin's financial concerns.

Many actors avoid reading critics comments about their work; they know that their minds will by-pass a hundred glowing reviews to fixate on just one stinker. From this moment onwards, Vincent could not escape the belief that at least eighty people in Arles were severely opposed to him. Such a burden is not easily lightened by dropping the number from eighty to thirty, or by speculating how many were coerced or just signed because acquiescing was easier than declining. Petitions never show how many people refused to sign, nor with what vehemence. I can imagine his friends trying to reason with him in this manner, but could any number of warm relationships truly insulate him from such a chilling emotional blast? In the

---

[84] Bernadette Murphy painstakingly analysed each signature, cross referencing the names with local marriage registers and her personal database of Arlesian residents for the period 1888-90. She has discovered that the thirty were all associated with each, as friends, work colleagues and witnesses at each other's weddings (Chapter 18, 'Betrayal', *Van Gogh's Ear*, Vintage, 2016).

March of 1889, Vincent went to some pains to ensure that his neighbours were not among the eighty petitioners.[85] In May, he wrote that people rarely talked to him when he painted outdoors.[86] In September, now in the asylum at Saint-Rémy, he expressed a new anxiety to Theo, borne out of his inability to comprehend why so many people had turned against him.

> 'It is very serious that wherever I might end up for any length of time, I would possibly have to deal with popular prejudices – I don't even know what these prejudices are – which would make my life with them unbearable.'
>
> Letter **604** (800), to Theo 5 or 6/9/1889

Soon after, he reproached himself for cowardice and, alarmingly, he fantasised about taking a revolver to the petitioners and to the Gendarmes who had locked up his 'Yellow House'.[87]

We thus see how the damaging echoes of this petition continued to reverberate within him. I propose that the petitioners' act was worse than the Levite's neglect of the wounded man, equivalent to finding an already wounded man by the roadside and administering a kicking. If any come close to being 'the robbers' in van Gogh's story, it is these petitioners.

The art world at large

The art world, the dealers, the critics, the exhibition organisers and the wider public mostly passed by on the other side from Vincent, at least in his lifetime. Contrary to the popular myth, he did sell some work, a few drawings and one oil painting. He also had a 'rave review'; Albert Aurier, writing in the *Mercure de France*, praised:

---

[85] Letter **582** (753), to Theo 29/3/1889.
[86] Letter **589** (767), to Theo 2/5/1889.
[87] Letter **605** (801), to Theo 7 or 8/9/1889.

'… the naïve truth of his art, the ingenuity of his vision, …

… the brilliant and dazzling symphonies of colours and lines …

… his profound and almost childlike sincerity, his great love of nature and of truth – his truth, his own truth.'[88]

This was written just seven months before Vincent's death. He read it and thanked the author profusely, sending him a study of some cypress trees – a valuable gift which would surely fetch millions of dollars at auction today. This review appears as one of the first cracks in an art world that, thus far, had shown Vincent only its stoniest face. One hundred and thirty years after his death, great crowds of the art-loving public are willing to queue outside in the rain to view his exhibitions. Yet in his lifetime he had to scrabble around to find anyone willing to pose for him.

He set out his frustrations in a letter to his mother. He offers her a distinctly Dutch analogy, comparing the art world with the seventeenth-century financial fiasco, 'tulip mania':

'And those high prices one hears about, paid for the work of dead painters who were never paid like that whilst still alive, it's a sort of tulip mania where the living painters get more disadvantages than benefits. And like the tulip mania, it too will pass. One can argue however that although tulip mania is now long gone and forgotten, the flower growers are still with us and will remain so. And that is how I see painting; which endures like flower-growing. And for that reason, I count myself fortunate to be in it.'

Letter **612** (811), to his Mother c. 20-22/10/1889

At this later stage in his life, Vincent seemed resigned to the fact that his talent would remained unrecognised. He would nevertheless

---

[88] 'Les Isolés: Vincent Van Gogh' G.-Albert Aurier, *Mercure de France*, January 1890.

continue to grow his flowers, disregarding the whims of the wider world. The Levite is a walking metaphor for this fickle art world. They are both presented with a scenario of momentous importance; they see and yet fail to grasp their best next move and so pass by on the other side, leaving future generations to shake their heads, forever critical of their poor judgement.

Van Gogh's view of life (the antithesis to 'passing by on the other side')

We have already seen how Vincent refused to 'pass by on the other side' when he met Sien. He never published a booklet of advice, containing his thoughts on life and how best to get through it, but the following two points can be gleaned from his correspondence.

'Fall in love'

In a letter to his sister Wil, Vincent offers her some advice. He tells her to fall in love and to fall in love many times, since committing great follies is preferable to studying. He proposes that those consumed with passions for religion, justice or art might be less serious, less saintly than those who fall in love. So it would be better for her to enjoy herself as much as possible and then whatever art or literature comes from her life will be alive. Context is important here: he wrote all this in 1887 when he was staying with Theo in Paris and, from what scant accounts we have, he was living a very full, if rather unhealthy life.

In the same letter, he created the following analogy for Wil, likening a human life to a grain of wheat. Each has the potential to grow into something wonderful, but too many simply wind up caught between grinding millstones:

> 'Now comparing people with grains of wheat – there resides in every human, who is healthy and natural, the power to germinate, just as in a grain of wheat. And germinating *is* natural life.

The power of germination within a grain, is what love is within us. Now I find us, standing around with long faces or fumbling for words, stymied in our natural development and prevented from germinating and placed in a situation as hopeless as that of grain caught between millstones.'

Letter **W1** (574), to Wil, Summer or Autumn 1887

He continues, insisting that Wil should not be crushed by 'melancholy and pessimism' and that her best way of escaping these was to hold determinedly onto her self-confidence and love. He had the insight to recognise that this course had not always worked well for him. All the same he refused to surrender to these two millstones and continued to rejoice in his 'impossible and highly unsuitable love affairs'.

Slap paint onto a blank canvas (or 'Make good art')

It was Martin Luther who originally advised his congregation to 'sin boldly' in 1521. Bloggers and scholars still argue about exactly what he meant by this. Van Gogh could have contributed to this debate. He despised mediocrity. He considered it far preferable to risk a mess, than to play safe and produce something bland. This brings us back to his lengthy correspondence with Theo about saleability. He refused to produce work simply on the basis that it would sell; he might as well be a hotel waiter as a mass producer of Italian style watercolours.[89]

In a letter to Theo at the beginning of October 1884, he illustrated this philosophy with an analogy where life is like a fresh canvas whose blankness is both stifling and scary. The best way to counter such fears is to start slapping paint around, without worrying too much about the inevitable mistakes:

---

[89] Letter **R13** (267), to van Rappard 18 to 19/9/1882.

'I tell you, if someone wants to be active, they must not be anxious about doing something wrong and must not fret about making the odd mistake. Many people think they will become good simply by doing no harm – but that's a lie and you used to say so yourself. That way leads to stagnation, to mediocrity.

When you see a blank canvas, which stares back at you with a certain imbecility, just slap something on it.

You don't know how paralysing that is, that stare from a blank canvas, that says to the painter, "You can do nothing". A blank canvas has an idiotic stare which so mesmerises some painters that they too become idiots.

Many painters are afraid of the blank canvas but the blank canvas is afraid of the true, passionate painter who dares – and thus shatters the mesmerising "You can do nothing".

Life itself continually presents a person with a blank page, a discouraging, and hopeless-making infinite emptiness on which nothing is written, as null and void as a blank canvas.

But however meaningless and vain, however dead life presents itself, the person of faith, of energy, of warmth, who's got a bit of nous about them, won't allow themselves to get flummoxed. He strides in and takes action, and hangs on to that, even breaking it, some might say "violating" it … But let them chatter on, those cold theologians.'

Letter **378** (464), to Theo 2/10/1884

Both Levite and Priest are destined for van Gogh's most searing indictment: that of mediocrity, the inevitable consequence of living without passion. They are clearly flummoxed by the half-dead man. Were either one a 'person of faith, of energy, of warmth, who's got a bit of nous about him', he would stride over and help. Compare the Samaritan's bright and clear lines with their muted colours. How does anyone end up so dull? Again, van Gogh has a theory, which he offers to Theo:

'How does someone become mediocre? By conforming and complying, from one day to the next, with the world's demands and by never speaking out against the world and by always yielding to public opinion.'

Letter **347** (414), to Theo 17/12/1883

He preached the value of making a stand, of refusing to compromise even if that meant being a nuisance. The author Neil Gaiman said something similar as he narrated his artistic journey for the commencement address at an American university.[90] He did not attend a four-year course. He just started writing and, the more he wrote, the better he wrote. Too many rules would have stifled him. He reasoned that if there were rules he needed to know, he would find them as he went along. He failed. He grew a thicker skin. He got discouraged. He carried on. One good rule that he picked up was not to write for money. His best writing is always the writing he is proud of. If it sells, well and good. If it does not … well he still has a piece of work that he is proud of. You can find his full speech on YouTube. It runs just shy of twenty minutes and it is well worth the listen. He ends with the impassioned instruction, 'make good art'. This sits well alongside Vincent van Gogh's advice about slapping paint onto blank canvases.

The Levite who passes by on the other side is related to all those who back away from a blank canvas, under the delusion that they will 'become good simply by doing no harm'. Fear prompts us to do a variety of strange things, one of which is producing bland work. Van Gogh has no truck with such thinking. He lives the antithesis. He strides in. He risks the mess. He shuns the dread of ridicule. His closing line about 'those cold theologians' tied all of this in with his feelings about formal religion. In his mind, theirs was a sterile world filled

---

[90] Neil Gaiman, Commencement Address May 2012, University of the Arts, Philadelphia.

with mutterings about violations. He himself had once lived like that, but could no longer. Instead, he lived as he worked, 'slapping' many tubes of paint onto hundreds of blank canvases. All of his work is now extremely valuable. Most of it is utterly breath-taking. In my opinion a small proportion is not all that great. Like any creative person, he had his misses as well as his hits. But even his 'misses' could never be called mediocre. And his 'hits' really are astonishing – truly astonishing.

Some further thoughts arising from
The Levite

Our place in other people's stories

Suppose for a moment that the Levite is not a fictional character ... or at least that his story continues and, when he reaches Jericho, his wife asks him how his day went. He replies, *'It was fine ... a bit scary of course but that's just the usual for that road.'* He then chuckles, *'And fine is fine, I didn't need it to be eventful. Excitement on that trip always means something bad.'* She laughs along and they sit down to their meal. If he has done his 'staring-at-the-road-and-focusing-on-that-and-that-alone' properly he might have entirely erased from his memory the image of a wounded man in the gutter. If so, the encounter will not merit so much as an entry in his diary. He will go to bed with no idea about the role he has played and would be baffled to discover that he is now firmly fixed as a character in someone else's story.

Suppose for a moment that we could pop back in time and chat with Mauve and Tersteeg. We might ask them for their opinion as to which of their contemporaries will 'make it' as artists, meaning by this, *'Which will be revered in years to come?'* They would no doubt reel off several names but Vincent van Gogh's would not be one of these. Our job as time-travellers is not to give too much away, so we keep schtum about the dedicated museum next to the Rijksmuseum and the eye-watering prices his paintings now attract. Mauve might secretly be hoping that his work would still be appreciated. It is; he was a great artist. But it is not for us to drop the bombshell, that he, Mauve, *is* remembered, but mainly as a minor character in a far more famous story called 'the life and times of Vincent van Gogh'.

105

Likewise, were we to visit Arles in early 1889 and find a petition thrust in front of us, we might wish to let slip a few truths that had yet to become true. As we refuse to sign, we must also resist telling how Arles will grow in fame precisely because this 'mad Dutchman' briefly made his home here. The night café where he drinks will be named after him, and countless future artists will set up easels on the banks of the Rhône, trying to capture his unique magic with reflected stars.

This encourages me to re-evaluate my encounters with people. Naturally, I expect to be the principal character in at least one story (my own life) and hope to be a major character in some of my friends' lives. There are many more stories in which I have a walk-on part, a brief cameo, or appear as an unnamed extra in the background. I, like the Levite, might already feature in some great tale of which I am largely unaware. *'I did what? Really? When was that?'*, my perplexed future self would ask. We have minimal control here. Posterity decides whose lives are memorable, for what actions and to what degree. I doubt Mauve and Tersteeg would be delighted to discover themselves unwittingly cast in the role of 'someone who failed to notice a genius'. Gauguin attempted to ensure posterity portrayed him favourably by writing an autobiography.[91] In this he painted a kinder self-portrait than other records allow, whilst making claims about van Gogh that are hard to substantiate, such as his fondness for absinthe, his violent behaviour and, perhaps most outrageously, that his great artistic debt was ... to Gauguin, whose teaching and techniques are evident in his best work – apparently.[92] In this, Gauguin forgot that Vincent had already

---

[91] *Avant et Après*, Paul Gauguin, Les Éditions G. Crès Et Cie, Paris, 1923.

[92] Vincent believed (and many agree with him) that much of his best work came from the Summer of 1888, a time he later called 'the yellow high note' (Letter **581** (752), to Theo 24/3/1889), when he painted many works, including ' The Night Café', 'The Yellow House' and 'Starry Night over the Rhône', as well as a couple of pictures of Sunflowers. All this was done *before* Gauguin arrived, which rather invalidates the latter's boast.

painted some of his greatest pictures, reaching his 'yellow high note'[93] in the summer of 1888, before Gauguin arrived on the 23rd of October. We cannot dictate how we will be remembered, but our best path for avoiding negative casting is not rewriting the past but acting with kindness in the present.

This all sounds rather vainglorious. Why, out of over seven billion people alive today, should there be any surviving memory of you or me in a hundred years' time? This would be pure vanity were it not for the belief in a God who values every human and remembers every human story. History might well forget us, as it has the vast majority of those who have gone before us. God will not. In God's accounts, we have some major roles in a very few narratives and some minor roles in a few more. Winston Churchill played a dramatic role in millions of human stories. Historians still argue whether he was more often hero or villain. The final say belongs neither to him, nor to posterity but to God alone. God sees and values the story of every person, the high, the mighty and those abandoned in the gutter; those whom we almost stopped to help – but then forgot as we hurried on to our next pressing engagement.

What we see and what we miss

Van Gogh was by no means immune from missing something of key importance, despite it being right in front of him. There is a great irony here; he was a man who dedicated his life to the observation of the world around him, but, even so, there was much he failed to notice. His paintings are testimony to his outstanding ability to see people and things which were worth painting: two women working alongside each other in a field, a stand of irises, a chair, a bedroom, a hallway in an asylum, and so on. His letters at times betray his incredible talent for not seeing certain things. In the July of 1882 he was still unable to countenance the simple fact that Kee Vos did not

---

[93] Letter **581** (752), to Theo 24/3/1889.

love him. He wrote to Theo in a puzzled mood, as one seeking enlightenment:

> 'Was Kee Vos right in disliking me? Was I completely deluded in persisting? I declare, I do not know. And it is not without pain or sorrow that I reflect on this as I write. I so wish I could understand better why Kee Vos acted as she did and also why my parents and hers were so steadfast in their ominous opposition to it – less through their words – but certainly these as well – than through their total lack of genuine, warm, living sympathy.'
>
> Letter **212** (244), to Theo, 6/7/1882

Kee Vos's words, 'No, never, ever', were arguably clear enough, but passion often provides its own blinkers. This can be positive, when dedicating all our energies to finding a place of safety, or hunting down a single objective, or finding the exact shade of yellow to paint that sunflower. We might have the whole of 'Kubla Khan' had Coleridge rejected his neighbour's distractions. Everyday life, however, rarely calls for such an extreme focus.

All too often we see only what we want to see. C. S. Lewis and Alan Bennett both suggest that our reading of books is less to change our minds but more to confirm what we think we already know.[94] A fun question, therefore, to lob into a discussion is, *'When did you last read something that completely changed your mind?'*

We can preen ourselves that we are fair-minded, adaptable, open to both reason and new ideas. The truth is more that we are frequently drawn to narratives that exonerate our actions, while imputing less than flattering motives to our opponents. If we can see that van Gogh did not have the full picture about Kee Vos, even when he had calmed himself into a more reflective

---

[94] *The Uncommon Reader*, Alan Bennett, Faber & Faber 2007, and *The Four Loves*, C. S. Lewis, Fontana Books, 1963

frame of mind, can we 'see' that the same is, at times, true for us? Dare we risk identifying those murmurs of self-will, even when the storms of our passions have subsided?

I would like to offer two examples of this disconnection, between our unique perspective and the view open to others. One is biblical, the other personal. The personal first: I once had the incredible experience of snorkelling at the Great Barrier Reef. In the first session, I moved with agile grace, as if flying over a magical landscape. There were submerged mountains, deep ravines and open sandy plains. All around me were fish of the brightest colours, darting through the fronds of the coral, in and out of the waving anemones. At one point, I saw a giant clam, far below me on the sea bed. Its many tiny blue eyes registered my passing shadow and it closed its mouth. I felt like an angel on an adventure or a minor god exploring a new domain. That was my perception. The view from the boat told a different story – one of several lumpen tourists, lying face down in the sea, sheathed in unflattering black anti-stinger onesies, clumsily slapping the surface with pink and yellow flippers. By my second dive I realised, having seen others, the massive gulf between my perception and my appearance to an onlooker. I was like a 'dad dancer' at a family wedding, lost in my moment and 'feeling groovy', whilst looking anything but.

This is all a bit negative. The message cannot always be that others will perceive our excitable selves as graceless clods. A biblical story flips this around. When Moses came down from the mountain, beaming with light because he had been speaking with God, those who saw him were alarmed. His face was shining so brightly that they begged him to veil himself. The key thing is, Moses had no idea what they were talking about; he did not know his face was shining.[95] Sometimes, when we are contentedly being ourselves, enjoying God and the life God gives us, we too might shine and yet be unaware of it.

[95] Exodus 34:29.

Our perspective on any incident is simply that; it is ours. We cannot claim to hold the definitive version. We only have 'our' take. We will see much and, at the same time, also miss much. We delude ourselves if we imagine we see everything. As onlookers, we can frown at Mauve, Tersteeg, the Arlesians petitioners and the all-too-slow art market; we can blast both Priest and Levite for any number of foul, cowardly motives, but in truth we will never know all the details of theirs or any other person's story. Where there is judging to be done, God alone is fully qualified. Only God sees our every act *and* our every omission. Only God understands all perspectives, including our own. It is also worth noting that Vincent was not one to hold grudges; it seems he was able to forgive past hurts and move on.

Recognise the human

The important thing is to try and keep on trying, to recognise the human. When we walk down a city street littered with cocoon-like sleeping bags, when the news shows us pictures of overfilled dinghies bobbing across the Mediterranean, when a teenager is being harassed online for their different take on gender identity, we do well to see through the headline and beyond any fear-mongering, and instead recognise the human being: inside the sleeping bag, on the precarious boat, or struggling within a body that feels alien.

For a while van Gogh sought to drum into Theo his mantra, 'sorrowful yet always rejoicing'. The mantra I seek to instil into my days is, 'recognise the human'. I am convinced that were I to manage this successfully, I would walk less as the Priest or Levite and more as the Good Samaritan.

Luke records another parable in which a vulnerable man is neglected.[96] Dives (the rich man) lives the good life, ignoring Lazarus who languishes outside his door. Dives presumably passes by Lazarus every time he leaves his house, but he gives

---

[96] The Parable of the Rich Man and Lazarus, Luke 16.19-31.

him nothing, not even the scraps from his table. The only beings who offer him God's kindness are the dogs who lick his wounds. This story has a wider scope than that of the Good Samaritan, where the drama is contained in a single day and we can only guess what becomes of the Priest and Levite. Dives and Lazarus's tale extends beyond this life into the next, where it becomes starkly clear that God never failed to recognise Lazarus's human worth and required Dives to do the same.

A parable in Matthew is closely related.[97] Jesus describes the day of judgement. It will all boil down to just one question. We, the judged, might be confused by the final outcome but for the Judge it will be as obvious as the difference between sheep and goats. That one question is not, *'Did you keep your life pure and free from sin?'*, or, *'Were all your religious doctrines correct?'*, or even, *'Did you sell all your possessions to secure your salvation?'*. The one question will be, *'Did you treat the least of your brothers and sisters well?'*. Christ accepts all acts of goodness to the least as if they are done for him personally. We are not always required to recognise Christ in these, 'the least'. All we need to do is first recognise a fellow human and then proceed with kindness.[98] The most aspirational example of this is the subject of our next chapter.

[97] The Parable of the Sheep and the Goats, Matthew 25:31-46.

[98] For a much fuller discussion about this, see Chapter 6 of *Simplicity* by Richard Rohr, The Crossroad Publishing Company, 1991.

CHAPTER 6

The Samaritan

'But a Samaritan while travelling came near him; and when he saw him, he was moved with pity. He went to him and bandaged his wounds, having poured oil and wine on them. Then he put him on his own animal, brought him to an inn, and took care of him. The next day he took out two denarii, gave them to the innkeeper, and said, "Take care of him; and when I come back, I will repay you whatever more you spend."'

Luke 10:33-34

Van Gogh's painting

Van Gogh's Samaritan struggles with every fibre of his being to raise the wounded man up and onto his animal. The two figures are locked together in combat, but not against each other. Their fight is in the eternal battlefields of life against death, of leverage against gravity and of hope against despair. They are not comrades supporting one another. This is no shared, mutually supported task. The fight is all the Samaritan's. The wounded man is completely unable to cooperate. If anything, his unconscious deadweight is colluding with all the forces that would drag them both downwards. His limbs spill out with unexpected lurches, threatening an already precarious balance, which the Samaritan just, but only just, maintains.

There is little dignity in the Samaritan's endeavour. He is no swan, gliding through his task with the semblance of ease, all effort hidden below the surface. His face is crushed. His cheek has been shoved around, squashed onto his own shoulder. His mouth is open just wide enough for him to gasp some air. That breath will be difficult since his chest is flattened by the weight of the stranger's torso. His sleeves have been rolled up to reveal his straining forearms. No doubt his spine is protesting at the contortions required. His sharply delineated left leg is locked, possibly shaking as he raises his right, in the hope of nudging upwards, with his knee, one of the wounded man's flopping limbs. His feet skid around in loose slippers, entirely unsuitable for the task. I imagine a mental scream coming from under his scarlet turban, '*Abandon, abandon! Stop this now, before you do yourself a serious injury!*'.

There is nothing complacent about this rescue. It requires the Samaritan's total engagement and he commits his entire being to its completion. He reserves no energy for his own protection, should the robbers return. In the moment caught by the painting, he is even more vulnerable than the wounded man was before the initial attack; the latter at least had his hands free to defend himself.

Looking beyond the Samaritan, we see that he has left his possessions wide open; proving that he has goods to steal and almost inviting the robbers to return. He cares not. He has acted in haste, rummaging frantically for wine, oil and anything that can be torn to make a bandage. After all, this is just 'stuff', and 'stuff' is only worth anything in the moment when it is needed. His attention is focused entirely on that which has real value: a wounded human in dire need.

Van Gogh has dressed the Samaritan predominantly in yellow, the colour of his wheat fields, his sunflowers and his sunrises. He may or may not have known Delacroix originally gave the Samaritan a red tunic. Either way, his choice is still deliberate. For him, yellows and golds were all about life. When describing another work, he states that a flood of pure gold sunlight takes away all sadness, even from death.[99] He named a time of great productivity the 'yellow high note' of his painting career.[100] He also believed painters should indicate a character's holiness not with a halo but rather with radiant, vibrant colours.[101] He explained to Theo the highly-focused effort required for the glowing yellows of his sunflowers; we can see his yellow-clad Samaritan working with similar passion to save the wounded man:

> 'Now to raise sufficient heat to melt those golds and those flower tones – it's not just any newcomer who can do that – it takes an individual's entire concerted energy and concentration.'
>
> Letter **573** (741), to Theo 23/1/1889

Not 'just any newcomer' could paint like Vincent and, as we shall see in the next chapter, not just any newcomer, in fact only one person, could truly be as good as this Samaritan.

---

[99] Letter **604** (800), to Theo 5 or 6/9/1889 – the picture he referred to is 'The Reaper' (F 619 / JH 1792).

[100] The 'yellow high note' came in the Summer of 1888, Letter **581** (752), to Theo 24/3/1889.

[101] Letter **531** (673), to Theo 3/9/1888.

Van Gogh's 'Good Samaritans'

In the preceding chapters, we considered who might have come into Vincent's mind as he painted each figure. We ask the same of his Samaritan. There are a handful of people who went out of their way to support him, such as, in Arles, the Reverend Mr Salles, Dr Felix Rey, the Roulin family and, in Auvers-sur-Oise, Dr Gachet. They are all important, but here we will focus on two other candidates. Only one of these is likely to have occurred to Vincent and that is his brother, Theo. The second, his sister-in-law, Johanna van Gogh-Bonger, played the hugely significant role that made his legacy available for millions today. Vincent never knew anything about this, because her work began only after his death.

Vincent's brother, Theo van Gogh

Without Theo, Vincent could not have become an artist. Raw talent, extreme dedication and an extraordinary feeling for colour and tone were all vital components in making Vincent the painter he was. These, however, were not enough. Try as he might, Vincent could not live by art alone. He needed money for food, clothing, medicines, shelter, canvases, brushes, ink and paint. This is the harsh note of practical reality that drains the romance from the artistic life; much as questions of gravity, or the need for fuel, dampen a good science-fiction fantasy.

Some artists find patronage from a wealthy enthusiast. Some marry a rich spouse. Others manage to structure their lives to incorporate part-time jobs to cover the basics. Vincent was too much an all-or-nothing character to juggle his painting with waiting on tables or, as L. S. Lowry, collecting rent. He was unable to find any sort of suitable wife, let alone a rich one. This left him in need of a sponsor. His parents offered some help, but the main respondent was his younger brother. Theo was far from wealthy but he was generous with what he had. Vincent's letters to him often contain requests such as:

'I have received the 10 tubes of white, but I'll need, as soon
as possible another dozen zinc whites
2 large tubes of Cobalt
1 " " Emerald
1 " " Chrome
1 small tube of Carmine
as there are some beautiful autumnal effects to do.'

Letter 608 (806), to Theo 28/9/1889

His letters are also filled with profuse thanks for all that had
already been given, mingled with guilt at what could not be
repaid. Vincent, for his part, tried to live as frugally as possible,
ever conscious that whatever money he had came from Theo.
In 1885, he told Theo that his plan was to go around wearing
clogs; 'il s'agit d'y aller en sabots', which meant being content
with a peasant's food, drink, clothing and accommodation.[102]
He had lived this way as an evangelist in the Borinage,
shunning all comforts. When his vocation changed, his ascetic
continued, coupled with an ever-growing sense of unease
as his success failed to materialise. The years went by, but
the expected sales did not come. He worked to a punishing
schedule, but no amount of effort on his behalf could conjure
the required response from the art world. At times he blamed
even Theo, accusing him of not trying hard enough to sell his
work or of patronising him with kind but useless critiques.[103]
But for the most part he was deeply grateful, even amazed at
Theo's continuing support.

Theo's struggles were considerable. He often found himself
caught in the cross-fire between his elder brother and their
parents. He also found sharing his Paris apartment with Vincent
nigh on impossible. Theo wrote to their sister Wil:

[102] Letter **400**, to Theo 13/4/1885.
[103] Letter **358**, to Theo 1/3/1884.

'My home life is almost unbearable. No one wants to come and see me any more because it always ends in quarrels, and besides, he is so untidy that the room looks far from attractive. I wish he would go and live by himself. He sometimes mentions it, but if I were to tell him to go away, it would just give him a reason to stay; and it seems I do him no good. I ask only one thing of him, to do me no harm; yet by his staying he does so, for I can hardly bear it.

...

It seems as if he were two persons, one marvellously gifted, tender and refined, the other, egoistic and hard-hearted. They present themselves in turns, so that one hears him talk first in one way, then in the other, and always with arguments on both sides. It is a pity that he is his own enemy, for he makes life hard not only for others but also for himself.'

Memoir of Vincent van Gogh, Johanna van Gogh-Bonger

Despite these frustrations, Theo loved his brother deeply and never doubted his talent or relinquished the hope of his paintings selling ... one day.

There is terrible sadness in Vincent's later letters, as all hope faded of ever making good on Theo's investment. The following was written to Theo in 1888, after Paul Gauguin had arrived at the Yellow House in Arles, bringing with him the prospect of some additional income:

And so I'm daring to hope that for you the burden will be a little less heavy and I'm daring to hope a lot less heavy.

As for myself, I feel I'm reaching the point of being morally crushed and physically exhausted, by the pressure to produce, for the simple reason that I have no other – no other way on earth of ever recouping what we've already spent.

I can't help it if my pictures don't sell.'

He then adds, with a hope which eventually came to fruition beyond the wildest dreams of either brother:

> 'The day will come however when people will see that they are worth more than the price of the paint and my living expenses.'

Letter 557 (712), to Theo 24/10/1888

As we know, with our gift of hindsight, his paintings are now ridiculously more valuable than their initial costs. Without Theo, they would never have been painted. Without Vincent's second Samaritan, they would never have become so famous.

Vincent's sister-in-law, Johanna van Gogh-Bonger

In April 1889, Johanna Bonger married Theo van Gogh. Their only child, Vincent Wilhelm, named after his uncle, was born the following year on the 31st of January 1890. Just one year later, Johanna found herself facing two devastating bereavements. Vincent had shot himself in the chest, dying two days later. Theo had also died, six months after his brother. Johanna was left with a baby, an apartment in Paris, a stack of letters, and a couple of hundred canvases painted by Vincent. At that time these were deemed financially worthless. They covered the walls of the bedroom, dining room and sitting room, and, to the great distress of her cleaner, were stored under the sofas, the beds and in every cupboard.[104]

Johanna turned this bleakest of situations into a global phenomenon. She worked on every useful contact she had in the art world. She collected and catalogued Vincent's correspondence. She arranged exhibitions. As early as 1892, Dutch newspapers were starting to repeat the name of Vincent van Gogh. In 1905, she organised his first solo exhibition at the Stedelijk Museum in Amsterdam, where four hundred of

---

[104] *Memoir of Vincent van Gogh*, Jo van Gogh-Bonger, December 1913.

his works, both paintings and drawings, were seen by over two thousand paying visitors. In 1914, she published her collection of Vincent's letters in both Dutch and German. She faced down several critics, since not everyone shared her enthusiasm for Vincent's work. She allowed all this to take precedence over her other great passion, the promotion of socialism. All this while she was raising her beloved son, struggling with her grief and juggling part time jobs to pay the bills. Later she arranged for Theo's body to be exhumed from his grave in the Netherlands and laid alongside Vincent's in the cemetery at Auvers-sur-Oise. They remain there to this day, side by side, their two graves covered by a single blanket of ivy.

Johanna died in 1925, leaving her son, Vincent, to continue her work. Mean-hearted people muttered that her motives were less about art and more about money. My answer to this is a question: *'Even if that were true, why would it matter? In what world does providing for a child, while seeking to rebuild a shattered life become a less than laudable motive?'* Besides, I do not believe that our life's achievements can ever claim one sole, pure motive. We are complicated and contrary beings. If we drill down honestly, we can always find a mixture of worthy and less than worthy reasons behind our actions. I consider Johanna's critics as living in some sort of fantasy world, untroubled by dull everyday realities such as rent, household bills and school fees.

Johanna seems at last to be gaining the recognition she deserves.[105] Hans Luijten published her biography *Alles voor Vincent* in 2019, alas only in Dutch.[106] Her diaries, however, can be found in English and online. One of many worthwhile entries indicates the depths of her fortitude; just over a year after Theo's death, she wrote:

> 'A letter from Toorop this evening that the exhibition in The Hague will be very soon … what a storm of emotions that'll provoke. We'll have to summon up all our courage before then – and be strong in the face of the attackers – because there'll certainly be many of them!'
>
> Johanna van Gogh-Bonger's Diary, 3 March 1892

According to her son, the publisher of Vincent's letters sent a wreath to her funeral bearing these three words, 'Faithfulness, Devotion, Love.'[107] Good words for this Good Samaritan.

The Samaritan in Jesus' parable

Why does the Samaritan act as he does? Jesus says that the Samaritan, on seeing the wounded man:

- 'was moved with pity' (NRSVA)

- 'had compassion on him' (KJV)

---

[105] 'Meet Jo' offers an excellent introduction to 'The woman who made Vincent famous' on the Van Gogh Museum's website (www.vangoghmuseum. nl). See also 'The Woman Who Brought Van Gogh to the World', Jess Righthand, smithsonianmag.com, 1 November 2010, and the final chapter in *Van Gogh in Auvers: His Last Days*, Wouter van der Veen and Peter Knapp, Monacelli Press Incorporated, 2010.

[106] *Alles voor Vincent: het leven van Jo Van Gogh-Bonger*, Hans Luijten, Prometheus, 2019. Hopefully this book will one day be published in English.

[107] Memoir of J. van Gogh-Bonger by V. W. van Gogh.

- 'his heart was filled with pity …' (Good News Translation)

- 'his heart went out to him …' (The Message)

Variants of the same Greek verb splagchnizomai (σπλαγχνίζομαι) appear in other gospel stories. Jesus feels this same tug in his guts, this same draw on his heart, when he meets a man with leprosy;[108] when he sees the crowds looking like sheep without a shepherd;[109] when a second crowd numbering thousands are hungry[110] and when he sees a widow at her own son's funeral.[111]

In Jesus' parables, it is given as the motive for a king releasing his servant from an impossible debt,[112] and for a father welcoming home his wayward younger son.[113]

We are familiar with the Samaritan. This story of his great compassion does not shock us. Jesus' first audiences, by contrast, are astonished. They know the storyteller's rule for three consecutive characters: the first two fail and the third succeeds. This was an established convention long before Goldilocks ever tried three beds and three bowls of porridge. They had their own three-part list: Priest, Levite and Israelite; this third character being your average Joe, a common, undistinguished, everyday type of person.[114] Their expectations shatter as Jesus delivers a switch, substituting a Samaritan for the expected Israelite.

His choice is deliberate. Samaritans were, in general, not popular with Jews. Ben Sirach views them with such hostility that he refuses to credit them even with the title 'a people':

---

[108] Mark 1:41.
[109] Matthew 9:36.
[110] Matthew 15:32.
[111] Luke 7:13.
[112] Matthew 18:23-35, see verse 27.
[113] Luke 15:11-32, see verse 20.
[114] See pages 102-103 of *Short Stories by Jesus*, Amy-Jill Levine, HarperOne, 2015.

'Two nations my soul detests,
and the third is not even a people:
Those who live in Seir, and the Philistines,
and the foolish people that live in Shechem.'[115]

The Wisdom of Ben Sirach 50:25-26

When Jesus is rejected by a Samaritan village, two of his more prominent disciples seriously propose, as an appropriate response, calling down fire from heaven.[116] Their planned retribution is totally disproportionate to the 'crime', if we can even call it that, but it undoubtedly points to a history of neighbouring peoples not living as good neighbours. Jesus enjoys an infinitely more reasonable conversation with a Samaritan woman at Jacob's well. As the two of them talk, they acknowledge the deep rifts between their two communities: each side claims to be the true descendants of Jacob and to know the correct place for worshipping God: Mount Gerizim for the Samaritans, and Mount Zion for the Jews. Jesus' disciples are astonished to find him talking one-to-one, not only with a woman, but with a *Samaritan* woman. To underline the extreme awkwardness of this encounter, John opens the whole narrative with this stark side note:

'Jews do not share things in common with Samaritans.'

John 4:9b

In short, a Samaritan is very far from the third character Jesus' audience expect. When he is first mentioned they might swiftly recalibrate their thoughts along the lines, *'So if the Priest and Levite both failed, how much more will this Samaritan?'*. But the Samaritan does not fail. His actions mend all those of the robbers.

---

[115] Shechem is an early name for Samaria.
[116] Luke 9:51-55.

The robbers	The Samaritan
1. stop and attack;	1. stops and cares;
2. inflict wounds;	2. binds wounds, pouring on oil and wine;
3. leave the man for dead, alone in the wilderness;	3. reclaims the man for life, putting him on his animal and taking him to safety;
4. steal money;	4. pays money for his care at the inn;
5. abandon their victim.	5. promises to return.

Van Gogh captures a key moment in this story. He tells us that the rescue demands the straining of every muscle and sinew in the Samaritan's body – a reversal, by one unlikely man, of all the efforts dispensed by a whole gang of robbers.

Some further thoughts arising from
The Samaritan

Finding safety

I have my bolt holes and, when I cannot visit them in person, I can usually find them with my mind. If I am frightened, I seek the familiar. If I am ill and abroad, I crave the dull routines of home.

Van Gogh found some sense of safety in the Yellow House, his home in Arles, and the first place he could truly call his own. He also found that the act of painting soothed his cares, very much as some people today can forget all else when fully immersed in sport, gardening, music, reading or gaming.

Jesus' wounded man awakes in the inn. Despite his aches and confusion, he understands that he is safe. This surely happens; the narrative implies that all ends well. We can imagine him opening his eyes and struggling to make sense of a window, the four walls and the strange furniture. Maybe the Samaritan is present and gently explains what has happened, reassuring him that in this new temporary home, all is well.

'Temporary' is a useful word when thinking about our usual bolt holes and any immersive activity. Painting and video games necessarily come to an end. Even the strongest sanctuary must eventually crumble. Besides, we would not want to stay there for too long, lest we lose confidence and start to feel besieged by the world outside. We should not lose ourselves too deeply in any positive activity, lest we become obsessed and engage with nothing else. Distractions and refuges work best when we treat them as temporary. Animals that have been caged for a short period cannot wait to escape. Those who have been locked up for months will back away from the opened door and huddle, trembling, in a corner. In the same way, our sense of what or where is safe can become woefully confused. The real world becomes too scary a place if we withdraw for too long. It is a tragedy if we ever look back at a former prison and find ourselves yearning for its familiar routines.

Ultimately for Christians, safety is neither a place nor an activity, it is a being; it is God. Ideally our relationship with God will not depend too deeply on locations, rituals or our own activity, but rather on God's grace. There are moments when we see, with unnerving clarity, the fragility of our existence; how it can be ended by just one accident, one illness or one set of robbers. We cannot live fruitfully at such an intense level every day but it is good to have an occasional reminder.

The Bible has many metaphors for the safety God offers. Some of these liken living with God to being in a physical place: a tower, a stronghold, a hiding place, a rock, a refuge, a fortress. My favourites are those which emphasise the relational. We are invited to see ourselves as chicks under the sheltering wing of our mother hen,[117] sheep guided through dangers by our shepherd,[118] orphans adopted by a loving parent,[119] widows provided for by a generous benefactor,[120] and displaced disciples who are personally escorted to an everlasting home.[121]

Religion becomes unsafe in all sorts of ways, whenever it loses sight of God. We can become unhealthily addicted to religious activities. We can find our hearts constricted if ever a religious institution becomes our sole locus of safety. We can grow fearful of love's messiness and unpredictability. We can become overly mindful of reputation. Van Gogh would readily concur. Remember how he dismissed so much church-talk as

---

[117] 2 Esdras 1:30, Matthew 23:37 and Luke 13:34.

[118] Psalm 23, Matthew 18:10-14, Luke 15:1-7.

[119] John 14:18, Romans 8:15, Galatians 4:4-6, Ephesians 1:4-6.

[120] Psalm 68:5.

[121] John 14:1-6.

'Jesuitisms'. Church people then compounded this damage by their reaction to his misadventures in love. In the end, he rejected all formal religion, but mercifully not all notions of God. From inside the asylum at Saint-Rémy, he wrote to Theo:

> 'I am not indifferent and in even in my sufferings, sometimes religious thoughts console me deeply.'
>
> Letter **605** (801), to Theo 10/9/1889

God is unlike any other refuge. Being hidden in God is not the same as losing ourselves in religious activity or retreating from the world and its woes. If anything, we find ourselves more attentive to those around us. A living relationship with God turns us both inwards, to be self-aware, humble and kind – and outwards, to engage lovingly with others. All the while drawing us ever Godwards, back, back and back again to God's loving embrace, our only enduring place of safety.

There are many pitfalls around religion, addiction being just one. I believe that our safest course is to approach God as a loving parent, and not as a respectable code of rules or some sanctimonious algorithm of behaviour, which guarantees our place in the afterlife.

Being in debt

Some people cope with debt better than others. A whole generation of students in England and Wales now find they have no choice about being debt-free; if they want to study, their only option is take out a student loan and so begin their careers saddled with thousands of pounds to repay. The days of full grants seem so idyllic as to be imaginary.

I sympathise with Vincent's dislike of being in debt. He was burdened by its weight. He constantly referred to his lurking dread of Theo regretting such an unwise investment. Like many fears, this had little foundation in reality. Theo remained devoted to Vincent and continued to believe in the worth of this project.

Truths such as these can allay fears but do not always completely disperse them. Anxieties often require frequent reassurances.

Christians find themselves indebted to God and cannot afford to be like Miss Charlotte Bartlett, in E. M. Forster's *A Room with a View*. She is most indignant. While chaperoning Miss Lucy Honeychurch on her first visit to Florence, she finds their rooms are not acceptable. Lucy's has no view. At dinner, the kindly Mr Emmerson proposes an exchange, arguing that he and his son have rooms they do not value and, if they swap, Lucy will have her view. Later Miss Bartlett explains her refusal to the kindly figure of the Reverend Beebe:

> 'I am, as it were,' she concluded, 'the chaperon of my young cousin, Lucy, and it would be a serious thing if I put her under an obligation to people of whom we know nothing. His manner was somewhat unfortunate. I hope I acted for the best.'
>
> 'You acted very naturally,' said he. He seemed thoughtful, and after a few moments added: 'All the same, I don't think much harm would have come of accepting.'
>
> 'No harm, of course. But we could not be under an obligation.'[122]

This makes we wonder, given her strong aversion to obligations, how Miss Bartlett gets on with God. If she struggles, she is not alone. I also wonder if the lawyer who prompts the parable might have similar issues; hence his questions about earning eternity. On paper, it is of course ridiculous to envisage how we as humans could ever have any other sort of relationship with God. If God creates, sustains and redeems all things, ourselves included, we can have no grounds for claiming anything as our own. In the Parable of the Rich Fool, Jesus explains the sobering

[122] *A Room With a View*, E. M. Forster, Chapter 1. Quoted with the kind permission of the Provost and Scholars of King's College, Cambridge and the Society of Authors as the E.M. Forster Estate.

truth that nothing is truly ours, not even our lives.[123] If God visited us as a generous alien, Miss Bartlett's brand of caution would be understandable. But God has gone to extraordinary lengths to avoid scaring us like this. God approaches us in the most familiar form imaginable: a human being. God is thus able to draw alongside us as one who understands our struggles intimately, even when our situation is dire and our needs more pressing than a mere room upgrade for a better view.

Being in dire need

Recognising our need for help is hard; the greater our need, the tougher this becomes. We might 'gift' the fulfilling of our smaller needs to another, building bridges of friendship in the process. However, when we are truly desperate we become reluctant to resort to the last hope still standing, because if that fails we will find ourselves facing desolation; sometimes it seems better to defer asking and thus preserve the illusion that all is not lost.

This thinking does not work well when applied to our relationship with God. Paradoxically, it is only once we acknowledge the inadequacy of our resources that we allow ourselves, finally, to be met by God. And God, like nature, abhors such emptiness and draws near to fill us. Perhaps this is the point of realisation that the tiny psalmist reaches, before the vastness of a starry night (Psalm 8 is surely one to resonate with van Gogh's admirers):

'When I look at your heavens, the work of your fingers, the moon and the stars that you have established; what are human beings that you are mindful of them, mortals that you care for them?'

Psalm 8:3-4

[123] Luke 12:13-21.

Perhaps this is also how the poor in spirit understand why they are called 'blessed', as Jesus says that the kingdom of heaven belongs not to the well-resourced, the self-sufficient or the self-assured, but to them.[124]

Vincent – a caged bird

In one of his most extraordinary analogies, Vincent explained how trapped he felt, back in 1880, during his seismic shift in vocation from preacher to painter. He likened himself to a caged bird whose torment contains several echoes of Jesus' Parable of the Good Samaritan.

'A bird in a cage in springtime knows all too well, that there is something he'd be good at, his strong instinct is that there is something to be done, but he is not able to do it. What it is, he cannot quite recall, apart from some vague notions and then he says to himself, "the others are building their nests and out making babies and raising their broods", then he bangs his head against the bars of his cage. The cage remains unscathed but the bird is maddened by pain. "Just look at that slacker!", says another bird as it passes by, "That one is such a freeloader." However, the prisoner lives on and does not die. There's nothing on the outside to show what's going on within; he appears well, he seems more or less happy in the sunshine. But then begins the time for migration – and with it a bout of melancholy – "but he has everything he needs in his cage" or so reason the children who look after him – but he's looking outwardly to the storm-swollen sky whilst feeling inwardly a mutiny against his fate. "I'm in a cage. I'm in a cage and I lack nothing? Idiots! Me, I have everything I need? I beg you, give me freedom to be a bird along with the other birds."

. . .

---

[124] Matthew 5:3 and Luke 6:20.

Do you know what makes the prison disappear? It's affection, every time, profound and serious affection – being friends, being brothers, loving each other – that's the powerful charm that opens the prison with sovereign power. Without this a person remains in death's grip. But wherever compassion is born anew, life is born anew.'

Letter **133** (155), to Theo 7/1880

Here, the children who trap the bird almost take the place of the parable's robbers; they do great wrong, only their sins come from ignorance instead of greed. And, rather than retreating from the frame, they remain present throughout. Fellow birds appear but then fly on, just as the Priest and the Levite pass by, offering no help. But what help could they bring? They have no power to unlock the cage. The caged bird is driven to self-harm, such is his frustration. Unlike the wounded man in Jesus' parable, he remains conscious throughout and by the end he is pleading for the one thing, he still believes can release him. And that is not money, family or fame, or even the freedom to pursue a vocation as a painter, it is love – an external gift of love:

Later in this same letter, Vincent wrote about love as something he needed to find first within himself, and then to bring to God, in the hope that this would somehow lead to God. My summation of this thought is: he viewed love as *his task* rather than as *God's gift*. And yet, at the end of his impassioned analogy of the caged bird, he calls on 'affection ... with sovereign power' as something from beyond both his cage and his resources, which nevertheless might find him, rescue and revive him ...

And, in my own words, I add: ... just as the Good Samaritan finds the wounded man, rescues and revives him.

CHAPTER 7

'Go and do likewise'

'Which of these three, do you think, was a neighbour to the man who fell into hands of the robbers?' The lawyer said, 'The one who showed him mercy.'

Jesus said to him, 'Go and do likewise.'

Luke 10:35-37

What happens next? Jesus has told his parable and Vincent has painted his picture. The wounded man is safely recovering in the inn. The lawyer has his answer . . . or at least an answer of sorts. He has Jesus' answer, which was not the answer he wanted or even a straight answer to his original question. Remember, 'Who is my neighbour?' was only ever a supplementary question, to clarify a point in his initial inquiry about eternal life. At the conclusion of his parable, Jesus asks him which of the three, the Priest, the

Levite or the Samaritan, was a neighbour to the wounded man. He replies, 'The one who showed him mercy'. Just as a side note, he does not name him 'the Samaritan', presumably that particular shock is still too raw. Jesus then says to him … and presumably to us as well:

'Go and do likewise.'

That sounds excellent. It makes great sense. We should be Good Samaritans to our neighbours in need, and when we say 'neighbours' we now understand that command has the most inclusive definition possible. 'Neighbours' are not just those living next door to us. They might not share our skin colour, nationality, age group, background, abilities, gender or sexuality. All they need to share with us, to quality for our best help, is our humanity. And if, along with loving God perfectly, we can be a neighbour of Samaritan-strength-quality to each of these, our place in eternity is assured.

I am taking a deep breath, because I am now going to attempt to argue:

1. That such an endeavour is impossible.

2. The Good Samaritan is a potentially dangerous model for us … if our question is 'How should we go out and do good to our fellow humans?'.

3. In telling this parable, Jesus is answering a different question; he answers the question he wishes the lawyer was asking.

The impossible endeavour

When I tried to 'Go and do likewise'

Remembering the Good Samaritan and Jesus' instruction to 'Go and do likewise,' I set off from home. I had plans to meet a friend at the cinema. Usually this would be a ten-minute walk, but this time I was delayed by the sight of a man in need. He was more slumped than sitting in the gutter, his lower body sheathed in a torn sleeping bag. Unlike the wounded man in Jesus' story, mine was conscious and so I started explaining how I planned to meet all of his needs. He told me to bugger off. The next man I met was more interested and allowed me to buy him a cup of tea. He then started exploring exactly what I'd meant by '*meeting every need*'. In no time at all I had handed over a considerable amount of money, which he assured me was for food and a place at the night shelter. He thanked me warmly and quickly disappeared off down a back alley, calling the name of someone who I presume was his friend.

Pretty soon there were many more candidates like him. In fact, I had managed to gather quite a crowd around me. I was living, after all, in a city in northern England at the end of a decade of austerity. By the time I had finally reached the cinema, my friend was long gone. I had meant to text her but, remembering how the Good Samaritan had given his all, I had donated my phone to someone with substantial needs. As it was, I no longer had any money for the ticket and I was feeling cold. My coat, hat and scarf were likewise no longer my own. I had hoped to feel the warm glow of satisfaction. Instead, I found myself fighting down some rather bitter thoughts ... '*That Samaritan had it easy. He had only had one wounded soul to tend. And what about tomorrow? I'll have to get up much earlier and walk to work by a different route, to avoid meeting any more poor needy souls.*'

As I arrived at home, I heard my landline ringing. It was my friend. She was angry with me. Not only had I stood her up but I had let her down. Earlier that day she had had a crisis at work and was worried she might lose her job. She had turned up, planning to postpone the film and instead just talk. When she had needed me, I had not been there.

I tell this made-up tale with a degree of flippancy to mask my awkward feelings of inadequacy in the face this instruction, 'Go and do likewise'. Jesus tells me all that the Samaritan did and then instructs me to do the same for all my neighbours in need

... and not just the nice ones. Whenever I have I set out thus, it is like walking on water. I sink at the first attempt and then scrabble back to safety, saving my sorry hide from drowning completely in the ocean of my new neighbours' needs. *'Surely this cannot be what Jesus intended?'* Yet he still says, 'Go and do likewise.'

You could try writing your own version of 'the day I set out to be exactly like the Good Samaritan to *all* in need'. I imagine that you too will not get that far from your front door before you realise the impossibility of your task. Even if you managed to be excellent to every homeless person, you would still pass by several heartbroken people, not to mention those struggling with hidden disabilities.

And our neighbours are no longer just those whom we physically encounter. Andrew Graystone writes in his book *Too Much Information?* about how this plays out in our increasingly inter-connected world.[125] The ocean of need around him grows wider each day. There are 4.4 billion people online, and all available for one-to-one contact with him. He is fantastically wealthy compared to most of these. He asks how he can be a good neighbour in this massively expanded neighbourhood, not just financially but also in terms of dignity. He concludes: he should not be evil, which in practice means no trolling, scaremongering, hiding behind multiple anonymous aliases or spreading false information. He proposes some guidelines for all of us: we take seriously our responsibilities around how we search, what we upload and what we download. We must never believe in victimless pornography. We should go online with love, both for neighbours and for ourselves (or, as he puts it, 'Love your self(ie)'). It is an excellent chapter in an excellent book, written with wisdom and wit. However, accepting Andrew's good advice is not the same as setting out with the intention of being as merciful as the Samaritan to everyone

[125] 'Who is my digital neighbour?', Chapter 6 of *Too Much Information*, Andrew Graystone, Canterbury Press, 2019.

in need. I am left asking what positive action I should take to alleviate the heaviness of Jesus' instruction 'Go and do likewise.'

Some other stories of those who tried – and failed to 'do likewise'

Compiling this list was worryingly easy ....

- An elderly woman fumbled for her purse at the Tesco checkout. By the time she had found it, the assistant at the till told her not to worry as her bill had just been paid in full by a stranger. She looked up and saw a man striding away, presumably glowing with pleasure at having performed a noble deed. The woman, for whom money was not a problem, later felt sad, wondering, 'Have I become so old? Do I really look so feeble?'

- A new church was being planted in a poorer part of a city. Some young, enthusiastic people moved into the community and started offering to 'help' the needy locals. They distributed leaflets introducing themselves and their 'servant ministry'. They proclaimed themselves ready to wash cars, mow lawns and even cut hair for free. There was no real take up for this. Some were bemused. The local barber was less than amused. Others grew worried about cults and brainwashing. Within three months none of this mattered, since they had all moved on. Apparently, God was now calling them elsewhere.

- People with impaired vision can suffer much from wannabe Good Samaritans. There was a sad story on the BBC about the perils of carrying a white stick on the London Underground. Trouble comes less from jostling crowds and rocking floors than from religious strangers who feel entitled to lay on hands uninvited and start praying for instant healing.[126] At the end of the day, when the white stick is folded up, the person, still visually impaired, asks, 'Will *I* ever be noticed for whom I am, or am I forever doomed to appear as a problem to be fixed?'

- People who use wheelchairs likewise can find themselves suddenly propelled along by a well-meaning stranger, who predicts their needs and pushes them to the destinations they think best. Such helpful souls might feel virtuous but the reality is, they have convinced yet another person that their wheelchair is their sole significant feature.

- Some 'charities' are run primarily as businesses. They provide 'voluntourism' opportunities for well-meaning people, seeking a positive-donor experience. Instead of being released into the wild, elephants are labelled as orphans and rich westerners pay to bathe them (despite elephants being quite good at washing themselves). And if we have concerns about enticing donors through maintaining elephants as perpetual orphans, how much more should we be concerned for human children kept in orphanages?[127] Charities can lose sight of their true purpose.

It seems that many who set themselves up as Good Samaritans either burn themselves out or lose themselves in dishonest self-delusions. One recurring theme here is sustainability. After all, how many elderly shoppers' bills can one man consistently pay? I have no wish to disparage good works; there are some incredibly kind, generous, wise and compassionate souls out there who do the most amazing things in the service of others. It may be the case that some of them draw inspiration from the Samaritan. I suspect their motivation is less the attainment

---

[126] 'Stop trying to "heal" me', By Damon Rose, BBC News 28 April 2019.
[127] See the work of the Lumos Foundation, www.wearelumos.org.

of a good eternity and more the rightness of helping another, and if questioned their self-awareness would prompt them to see themselves more often as Priests and Levites, than as the Samaritan.

Van Gogh as a Good Samaritan

In previous chapters, we have speculated over van Gogh's thought associations as he painted each character: the Priest – his father; the Levite – Mauve, Tersteeg and the petitioners of Arles; the Good Samaritan – Theo and Johanna van Gogh. We also wondered if, clean shaven as he was in 1890, he saw himself in the wounded man. Now I am asking whether he saw himself, or at least his younger self, in the Samaritan. The question is prompted by the colour of his beard; van Gogh gives him a russet beard, very much like the one he himself sported for many years. Delacroix's Samaritan has a dark brown beard. Possibly I am reading too much into this change. It might be that Vincent made an artistic choice or that he had simply forgotten Delacroix's palette; remember, he was working from a black and white lithograph. I think the question is worth asking, because we have already seen two quite extreme examples of van Gogh setting out to 'Go and do likewise'.

Van Gogh tried to be the perfect minister to the miners of the Borinage. His efforts met with a considerable degree of success. They remembered Monsieur Vincent as 'the Christ of the coal mines'. However, he could not sustain such an exhausting burden of neighbourliness. He did not look after himself properly and in the end his superiors stopped him after just six months before he crashed completely and did lasting damage to himself ... and others.

Van Gogh then tried to be the perfect saviour-husband to Sien. This relationship began with a noble act of rescue; he had refused to pass on by when he saw her desolate on the streets. His heart was filled with compassion. Unlike others, he recognised her as a human being rather than a prostitute.

He scorned the dangers, scoffing at the opprobrium of his parents and sought to provide for all her needs. At first his letters to Theo brimmed with righteous confidence; in the summer of 1882 he wrote:

> '... as for myself, I've always needed to love another creature and this won't ever stop. Preferably, I personally don't know why, an unhappy or spurned or abandoned creature.
>
> ...
>
> I've always believed that "Love Thy neighbour as thyself" is not an exaggeration but simply how things should be.'
>
> Letter **219** (250), to Theo 23/7/1882

However, within a couple of years his idealism was floundering on life's harsh realities. He had grown tired of Sien's poor habits and of her mother's constant interference. Eventually he left her for a sketching tour of Drenthe, knowing he would not return. There, he encountered other wounded souls. Again, compassion filled him but swiftly turned to melancholy as he recognised that their rescues were beyond his power. He explained this to Theo in the September of 1883:

> 'I see her [Sien] in them; her weakness and slovenliness only serve to heighten the likeness. I know that she is no good, that I am completely justified in acting as I do, that staying there with her wasn't an option, I couldn't bring her with me either, so what I did was clearly sensible, it was wise – or however you'd phrase it. But that does not stop it cutting right through me and melting my heart, when I see such a poor little figure, feverish and miserable.
>
> How much sadness there is in life.'
>
> Letter **324** (386), to Theo c. 15/9/1883

These were not isolated incidents. There were others, one of which belongs to the dreadful night of the 23rd of December,

1888. Van Gogh took his severed and wrapped ear to a local brothel, asking for a woman named Rachel. According to Gauguin, he gave it to her saying, 'Here you are, in memory of me.'[128] The newspapers recorded similar versions of these words, immediately recognisable to Christians, as being close to those spoken by Jesus at the Last Supper. Rachel, not a prostitute but perhaps a cleaner in the establishment, bore the scars of an attack by a rabid dog.[129] As a wounded woman, like Sien, she stirred van Gogh's compassion. I do not consider it beyond the bounds of possibility that his collapsing mental state revealed, close beneath the surface, an image of himself as a Christ figure. He offers her part of his broken body; a sacrifice which he believed, in his highly confused state, would benefit her. Why he chose his ear, we cannot know.

Van Gogh is not alone in discovering the impossibility of being a consistently good 'Good Samaritan'. Did he reflect on these and other awkward experiences in the spring of 1890, as he painted his red-bearded Samaritan? By this time he was certainly wounded, but did he still think of himself as a saviour figure? He had long since departed from organised Christianity but he continued to respect its beginnings. Back in 1884 he lamented the loss of its original potency but praised its founder as 'sublime'.[130] In 1887 he wrote a telling summation of his position in a letter to his sister Wil:

'As for me, I am always glad that I have read the Bible better than many people these days, just because it gives me a certain peace that once there were such lofty ideals.'

Letter **W1** (574), to Wil, summer or autumn 1887

---

[128] «Voici, dit-il, en souvenir de moi,» *Avant et Après*, Paul Gauguin, Les Éditions G. Crès Et Cie, Paris, 1923.
[129] Bernadette Murphy believes she has discovered Rachel's true identity (Chapter 20, 'Wounded Angel' *Van Gogh's Ear*, Vintage, 2016).
[130] Letter **378** (464), to Theo, 2/10/1884.

Were 'lofty ideals' all that was left to glean from the Parable of the Good Samaritan? 'Go and do likewise', would then translate as Jesus saying, '*Go and give it your best shot … but don't beat yourself too much up when you fail. I've deliberately set the bar too high for practical purposes. This is more for reference … a gold standard to which you can aspire but never hope to achieve.*'

A potentially dangerous model

If Jesus really meant us to take 'Go and do likewise' literally, as '*Go and do exactly the same as my Samaritan*', then he risks contradicting himself, both in his everyday practice and in his teaching.

Remember how the Samaritan proceeds:

- The Samaritan acts as a stand-alone hero. He requires no colleagues. He is omni-competent and arrives equipped with all the necessary resources to rescue this wounded stranger.

- The Samaritan's task is straightforward. The decision to help the wounded man is both hard and simple; hard because the effort required is immense and the risks high, simple because the wounded man's needs are obvious. Deeply wounded people are rarely helped so easily. They might opt for denial, deceiving themselves and others, rather than facing the truth of their situation. They might try to brave things out, preferring to soldier on alone and not be a burden. They can be defensive, aggressive, uncooperative, unreliable, untrusting, disruptive and manipulative. Those with very deep wounds may find it impossible to believe that someone will stick with them beyond the immediate moment of crisis, and spend many years 'acting out', testing the boundaries of all new relationships to breaking point.

- The Samaritan does not consult the one he rescues. It would be grossly unfair to use this as a criticism against him. He can do no consulting – Jesus has set up the story so that the 'patient' is unconscious. This 'set up' convinces me that his intention for this parable is something other than a generalised model of grade-A caring. For that, he would surely take a different approach; one where the patient is awake and their views can be sought, and their care designed accordingly.

- The Samaritan engages in a one-off act. Once the wounded man is patched up and safely in the inn, the task is pretty much complete – a full, perfect, and sufficient rescue. This comes down to the story's set-up once again: Jesus places only one wounded man on the road. His Samaritan does not meet the battered, unconscious guardian of three small children, who in terror have hidden themselves and are still at risk. He is not faced with a road littered with victims. He has no need to ration his resources to ensure that there is something for everyone. He is spared the agony of deciding which of many victims are those most likely to survive, and prioritising their care to the cost of the others. This is a luxury not afforded to all emergency workers.

In short, the Good Samaritan's rescue is not the best model for helping others. His methods serve as a wonderful template for those travelling alone through a wilderness and meeting just one unconscious victim, who has been attacked and left for dead within a day's ride of an inn. 'Go and do likewise' might be doable in that scenario, which is more extreme but less complex than walking through Manchester's streets on a cold winter's evening. But Jesus is not offering here the perfect answer to the request, *'Teach me, in practical terms how to do good to my fellow humans.'* His carefully constructed narrative makes an excellent answer to an entirely different question, to which we shall come in a moment.

Jesus himself does not work to this model of 'Going and doing likewise' in his daily ministry. He does not heal every sick person he meets; he chooses only one man from all those waiting

at the Sheep Pool.[131] Neither does he set out to abolish poverty
with one masterstroke, being realistic that there will always be
poor people in this world.[132] His usual praxis is collaborative.
He recruits a team and ministers alongside them.

Neither does Jesus teach his disciples to proceed like his
Samaritan. Certain elements appear consistently in this parable
and in his other instructions, such as compassion for the
downtrodden and sacrificial love for strangers, even enemies.
However, the Samaritan is not a practical embodiment of
everything else Jesus expects:

- Jesus sends out his followers to minister in groups; pairs
  being the absolute minimum.

- Jesus demonstrates how to engage with people, enquiring
  about the sort of help they want. He recognises the human,
  rather than the walking stick or the begging bowl. Some
  might think a blind person's needs are obvious but Jesus asks
  all the same.[133]

- Jesus warns his followers away from setting themselves up as
  omni-competent heroes, forbidding them such titles as 'rabbi'
  or 'father'. Rather they are to be humble, drawing alongside
  those in need, as servants.[134] Their focus should not be on
  accolades, privileged seats and special costumes, but rather on
  God's glory, as found through real encounters with others.[135]

- Jesus warns against being over-eager to sort out everyone
  else's problems. Someone who presumes to remove a
  speck from another's eye must first check for the logs in

---

[131] John 5:1-9.
[132] Matthew 26:11 and Mark 14:7.
[133] Mark 10:51.
[134] Mark 9:35, Matthew 20:26, Luke 22:26-27, John 13:5-16.
[135] Matthew 23:8-10.

their own.[136] Two essential keys for helping others are self-awareness and humility, neither of which are the usual prime attributes of superheroes.

- Jesus tells his followers that his burden is light and his yoke easy. He does not expect them to take full responsibility for the impossible and then burn themselves out.[137]

The Samaritan exists in a carefully set-up story. By no means does he defy Jesus' teachings about being kind – but *we* might, if we adopt his praxis as our sole template. He presents a model that could be damaging, both for us and those we seek to help. So why does Jesus invent *this* scenario and *this* character? What is his purpose, if it is not showing us how to be good?

The question Jesus answers ...

The straight exchange
If Jesus had been in the habit of giving straight answers to straight questions, the exchange might run like this:

The lawyer: 'Teacher, what must I do to inherit eternal life?'

Jesus: 'Nothing.'

The lawyer: 'Sorry ... I don't think I heard you correctly ...'

Jesus: 'I said "Nothing."'

The lawyer: 'Oh! So I did hear you correctly the first time ... Can you explain, because I thought you'd ...'

[136] Matthew 7:3-5.
[137] Matthew 11:28-30.

Jesus: 'You can't "do" anything, and you imagining
                  that you can only shows that you have a seriously
                  flawed concept of eternity.'

The lawyer: 'Are you saying, no one can be saved?'

Jesus: 'I am saying eternity comes only as a gift from
                  God, not as a reward for being good and
                  certainly not as any "payment" for doing some
                  one-off special good deed. Eternity is far too
                  valuable for that. So, if you want it, try asking
                  God and ditch any notion of earning your
                  ticket.'

This short exchange lacks finesse and had Jesus proceeded thus, Luke's Gospel would be a few verses shorter and we would be without one of his finest parables. Fortunately, Jesus rarely gave straight answers. In this case, he chooses to answer the question he wishes the lawyer had asked.

The lawyer's question does not deserve a straight answer because it is fundamentally flawed from the start. Eternity is far too precious to be earned or awarded as a prize. He is truly misguided if he imagines there is any one thing or set of things that he can *do* which will guarantee heaven's doors will swing open for him. If he maintains that he can fulfil all the commandments, he is deceiving himself. Loving God perfectly, without ever being distracted, is impossible for us. Hopefully we also see that loving *all* our neighbours in need, as the Samaritan loves the wounded man, is equally beyond our resources as individuals. The lawyer, however, seems determined to give this a go. So perhaps 'Go and do likewise' is Jesus' saying to the lawyer, '*Good luck with that. Give earning eternity your best shot and see how long you last … then maybe come back and we'll talk some more.*'?

The same logic can be applied to Jesus' instruction to the rich man, 'Sell all that you own and distribute the money to the poor, and you will have treasure in heaven; then come, follow me.'[138] We do not know if this rich man attempts this approach to eternity. But even if he successfully wrenched his wealth from his vaults, he must still return to Jesus *and then* follow him. Because salvation can only come as a gift from God, and never in recompense for our wondrous deeds.

Those who do not ask such flawed questions are spared such convoluted answers and instead find themselves simply invited to follow, without the additional obstacles of selling everything or living as perfect Samaritans. And as they meet Jesus and follow him, they find the grip of their material possessions naturally loosening, and the numbing delusions of self-righteousness surrendering to grateful humility.

'How can I be good to my neighbour?'

The lawyer could ask instead, 'How can I be good to my neighbour?' If the question is genuine rather than a test or trap, Jesus would surely welcome it and give a stunning answer. As there is no record of any such exchange in the Gospels, we can only speculate on what he might say. We could cobble together something through eavesdropping on his other conversations. But I doubt such a question would elicit from Jesus the Parable of the Good Samaritan. I am guessing he would say something else, maybe a new parable, exquisitely constructed to demonstrate the goodness of a servant's role.

In the same way, the rich man in Luke Chapter 18 could have asked Jesus, *'I realise that I'm holding quite a lot more money than other people. What's the best way for me to start sharing out what I have with those in need?'*. Again, no one ever says anything like this directly to Jesus. If they had, I am quite sure that his answer would not include quips about camels and eyes of needles.

Jesus has a habit of setting impossible standards, but only for those who wish to be told that they are beyond reproach. He

138 Luke 18:22b.

says that hating someone in your heart, even calling them a fool, carries the same sentence as murder. He is equally strict about adultery. We might protest, *'Well I'm more than fine on that one … unlike so many others …'*, but he continues: even looking at another with lust is essentially the same and equally damnable. He then launches into a series of instructions about tearing our eyes out … at which point we can be certain that he is not speaking literally.[139] I do not believe he says any of this to crush us. If he intends to crush anything, it is the foolish pride that insists we can make it on our own. When we hear him correctly, we immediately desist from every version of the self-destructive game called, 'Earning my eternity my way'. His impossible standards are given only to those who want to carry on playing, and thus preserve their right to look down upon others. To those who simply approach him with humble trust, he opens wide his arms and says, 'Come follow me.'

At the very end, on the cross, a dying criminal asks for his mercy. Jesus sets him no impossible standards. He makes no mention of his convictions or any other barrier to God's grace. The dying man likewise parades no proud boasts about his worthiness and so he receives the good words:

'Truly I tell you, today you will be with me in Paradise.'

Luke 23:43

'And how is God good to me?'

If the lawyer were to ask, 'And how is God good to me?' Jesus might well tell a story beginning, 'A man was going down from Jerusalem to Jericho, and fell into the hands of robbers …'. I believe that this is the question Jesus wants the lawyer to ask, and not, 'Who is my neighbour?', because this is the question Jesus actually answers. He often turns the tables like this.

How much we benefit from this parable, depends on the

---

[139] Matthew 5:21-30.

questions we bring. If, like the lawyer, we want to know what we must *do*, then we will look to the Samaritan, the Priest and the Levite, as both good and poor role models, to guide our conduct. If our questions are about God's goodness, we might risk seeing ourselves as the wounded man.

I have heard it said that, when viewing a group photo, the first person we look for is ourselves. The same can apply to stories; we ask, 'Who in this, is most like me?'. In a good parable, all the characters will reflect back to us something of ourselves. After a while we might say, *'I can relate to each of them at different times. But today I see myself the most in …'*. Usually we want the good guy's story to be our story, but hopefully we now see that the Samaritan sets a standard to which we can only aspire, rather than a pattern that is already ours. So, if not primarily in the Samaritan, in whom else might we find ourselves? Neither Priest nor Levite are immediately appealing, so how about the wounded man? Can we see ourselves in him?

- Dare we face our fragility and recognise how quickly accident, attack or illness can end our lives?

- Dare we confront the myths of our resourcefulness, along with those of our own 'Priests and Levites'? They might help us at times, but ultimately neither they nor we have the power to save us, when we are in such dire need.

- Dare we risk that glimpse of how very small we are in the context of eternity? How do we cope when we see our entire existence as limited to one small (and overheating) planet in an ever-expanding universe, and occupying only the very briefest of moments in the infinitely wider history of time?

- Dare we accept how utterly unable we are to earn any eternal significance?

If we take this approach and find ourselves in the wounded man, we will discover new depths to the words 'lost' and 'helpless'. And if it is too hard to see ourselves as less than a dot in space, in a fleeting moment of time, we can at least relate to a human robbed of everything, beaten up, stripped of all identity and now lying unconscious, left to die in the gutter. For any who recognise themselves as the wounded man, the question 'How is God good to me?' is extremely relevant, as is the answer given in the parable. If God is anything like the Samaritan, we will know that we are valued, despite our smallness, and found, despite the wilderness in which we are lost. We will also regard as arrant folly any notion of earning our significance. All comes from God alone. All comes solely as gift. There can be no other way.

If God really is as good as the Samaritan, God will find us wherever we are and will give generously to us, at great personal cost. God will come as a human, quite possibly as an outsider, who is not instantly recognisable but nevertheless, fully human. And yet this human will expend every fibre of their being to rescue us, revive us and bring us to safety. Look again at van Gogh's Samaritan. See the effort, the strain, the focus and the vulnerability and dare to believe that this is the very same passion God has for you. This parable, in answer to a question about eternity, is far more than an incident on a wilderness road. This is the story of how God is good to us.

There is an unwritten ending. We do not know what happens next for this lawyer. Does he take Jesus literally? Does he set out to 'Go and do likewise,' to emulate the Good Samaritan and attempt to be that perfect neighbour to everyone in need? Maybe he tries and deludes himself that he is succeeding … I hope not. Maybe, like van Gogh, he gives it a good shot only to discover the task is too 'lofty' … out of his reach but nevertheless admirable in its idealism. If so does he, like van Gogh, move on to concentrate on what he is good at? Vincent resolved to become a better painter. Perhaps he dedicates himself to becoming a better lawyer.

Salvation's story

There is another possible future. No doubt as time passes the
lawyer hears the news of Jesus' crucifixion and the rumours of
his rising. One record says that all Jerusalem was talking about
little else at the time.[140] Is it beyond the bounds of possibility
that he connects the struggles of Jesus with the exertions of the
Samaritan? The two men have much in common:

- Both appear as a mistrusted outsider, rather than as part of
the Establishment.

- Both bring God's salvation to those who have no
understanding of what is being done for them.

- Both place themselves at huge risk for the benefit of another,
giving their all at great physical cost. We see especially in van
Gogh's painting how the Samaritan bodily bears the burden
of the wounded man.

- Both 'recognise the human' and respond with compassion to
those in dire need.

- Both are filled with the kind of compassion that leads to
decisive action. The Samaritan risks his safety for a stranger.
Jesus lays down his life, for others, even his enemies.[141]

- Both demonstrate that love cannot remain as feelings but
must be realised in choices and actions.

- Both provide a concrete 'YES' to our desperate human
question, '*Despite our smallness, our helplessness, do we have
significance?*'.

[140] Luke 24:18.
[141] John 10:15-18 and Romans 5:7.

- Both give love as a rich personal gift, undeserved and unasked for; love so valuable that any notion of repayment or settling the debt is utter foolishness.

The ideal set by the Samaritan is too lofty for any individual human to reach … apart from one. Jesus is the exception to so many rules. His parables are not exact parallels. They are never intended to be. The Good Samaritan moves on, promising to come back later. Jesus also says he will return, but his 'moving on' is far more dramatic. He dies and returns by rising again whilst promising an even greater return at the end of the age.

If the lawyer finally makes this connection, he will have a good, if unexpected answer to his question, 'And who is my neighbour?'. Because if he can find his story in that of the wounded man, he will understand that, when considering eternity, his good 'neighbour' is not someone in need of his mercy, but rather the one who, in mercy stops for him.

My story?

I used to see the Parable of the Good Samaritan as a key story for me, because it led to the key commission, 'Go now and be as good as the Samaritan.' This was Jesus making my duty clear to me. This was far more daunting than that wonderful trio of 'lost' parables, which appear a few chapters later in Luke's Gospel.[142] The seeker's world stops, while sheep, coins and sons remain lost. The moment they are found all heaven erupts with rejoicing. I enjoyed these stories; they culminate not in a hard instruction but rather in a revelation of love so divine that it continues to surpass my wildest hopes.

The first two in the trio are full of encouragement, but I chose neither as *my* story. I counted 'the lost coin' as having the least significance for me. Coins go missing by accident, theft or

[142] Luke 15:18-31 The Parables of the Lost Sheep, the Lost Coin and the Lost Son.

their owner's neglect. They are entirely passive in the adventure. Sheep have a higher degree of agency but they do not rebel or scorn care. They merely go astray, happily wandering from one tempting sight to another. They can be lost long before the dreadful realisation hits them. Perhaps this comes at the bottom of a ravine, or when trapped in a thicket, or on catching the scent of a hidden, but keen-eyed enemy. So the lost sheep felt closer to *my* story; I could relate to one who dumbly daydreams its way into danger.

The third in the trio, 'The Parable of the Prodigal Son', was by far the most appealing. My then theological world preferred stories of wilful disobedience and salacious depravity. Most conversion testimonies were rewordings of the younger son's tale; giving our Heavenly Father the two-fingered salute and deliberately turning to our own way, to our sorry undoing and to his great cost.

In this quest for 'my story' I neglected three significant points. The third 'lost' parable contains not one but two lost sons. There is the better-known and easier-to-identify-with younger scallywag, but lurking out in the fields, is his equally lost elder brother. He is in even greater peril, having anaesthetised his self-awareness with self-righteousness. But in his own way, he insults his father's grace with scorn to equal his brother's. I became so invested in the younger son's story, it did not occur to me that the elder's could also be mine.

I also failed to understand that this was never 'all about me'. As a product of a highly-individualised culture, I forget all too easily Jesus' instructions require a collective response. If his call is to me, it is to me as a part of several wider families: Church, city, country and so on, up to the global community of all humanity. The call to 'go and do likewise' applies better to groups than to lone wannabe heroes.

My greatest error by far was to dwell for too long on my place in these stories and not on their true centre. One character dominates them all, whether as a caring shepherd, a diligent woman, a patient father or a merciful stranger. Each scenario gives us new insights into the same personification of salvation.

The Parable of the Good Samaritan is just as much as a 'Parable of the Lost' as are the later three. Is the wounded man like the coin? He has a similar degree of agency. He is not personally at fault and as one knocked senseless, he is unable to ask for his salvation. As such, his story is less appealing than the wild prodigal's. Even the sheep might be able to spin a better yarn. The truth is, none of this matters; these four parables tell us that there are many ways of becoming lost, maybe as many as there are people who have drawn breath. No one story can ever fit all. The relevant point is, however we got lost, there is one who comes to find us.

God's story

If my story reads, 'When I'm lost, God finds me,' then God's story is, 'God has come to seek and save the lost'.[143] He finds me near his house, wearing some raggedy scheme, to earn my keep and he calls me his child. He leaves a party to find me, when I am so bitterly lost that I am cursing him as a slave-driver. Again, he calls me his child. When I am the only one who is lost, she leaves ninety-nine to look for me, such is the value she places on me.[144] She does not stop searching for me, shining her light into the darkest corners until at last, I am safe again in her hands and then with wild celebration, she restores me to the place she has been keeping for me. Even if I am so lost that I am left for dead in a place where no other rescuers can help, God finds me, binds my wounds, hoists my unresponsive form onto his beast and takes me to safety, paying for my care and promising to return. This may be my story, even our story, but it is much more God's story; God's personified salvation comes to seek and save all who are lost, so that we can be found in God's story.

---

[143] See Luke 19:10.
[144] Shepherds can be female as well as male.

Jesus' parables as a work of art

We find ourselves back in Sunday School, where answering 'Jesus' is a fairly safe bet for most questions. We are asked, 'What's the meaning of this parable? Who is my neighbour?'. We reply tentatively, 'Is it ... Jesus?' And the reply is, 'Well yes ... and no ... and yes again ...' Jesus' parables are works of art and as such they contain many meanings and are open to a great variety of valid interpretations. We would lose much if we insisted on one focus, to the exclusion of all others. Even if we identify Jesus as the central core of the parable and rejoice that this is ultimately more God's story than ours, we cannot avoid other questions:

- How can we hear this parable and not see that all humans have immense value, and that every human in need is our neighbour? We can never justify ignoring another such human because they do not look like us, love like us, act, speak, believe or think like us.

- How can we fail to see our loved ones in a new light? If they are struggling with needs greater than our resources or if they should ever move beyond our help, we now know that God still sees them. Lost to us does not mean lost to God, who gives them a significance far beyond their collected atoms momentarily floating in time and space.

- How should we restructure our lives? What is a healthy level of trust for us to place in our human systems, philosophies, institutions and their personnel, knowing now as we do, that they alone can never save us?

- How can we live together, as those found in God's story, hearing this story of mercy and sharing the call to 'do likewise'?

Vincent van Gogh and the Good Samaritan

Real love can never exist in words divorced from action. Real love is seeing, feeling *and* doing. Love goes on. The story cannot end here. The Reverend Dr Martin Luther King, Jr. takes this train of thought further than most: he acknowledges our duty to the bruised and battered on life's roadside, but argues that a single act, such as giving a coin to a beggar, can never be enough. True compassion requires us to transform the whole Jerusalem to Jericho road for all travellers, along with every structure that leaves people in the gutter.[145]

The work of the Good Samaritan does not end at the inn. Neither does ours. This book, however, must come to an end. The last words by rights belong to Vincent van Gogh. In 1888, long after his 'religious phase' had ended, he wrote about Christ to his friend Émile Bernard. He recalls Christ's great power with words; his parables being the prime example. He refers to the sower, and surely does not choose the word 'prodigal' in ignorance of its resonances. I especially enjoy his quip about Jesus declaring his words would last forever whilst never deigning to write any of them down:

'This great artist – the Christ – even though he disdained from writing books about ideas and feelings – certainly felt considerably less disdain for the spoken word – and especially the parable (what a sower, what a harvest, what a fig tree etc.)

And who would dare to say that he was lying on that day when he so offensively predicted the collapse of Roman buildings and affirmed "heaven and earth shall pass away, but my words shall not pass away."

These words that he spoke as a prodigal great lord but did not deign to write down, are one of the highest summits reached by art, which in them becomes a creative force – pure creative power.

These considerations, my dear friend Bernard, lead us

[145] 'A Time to Break the Silence', Dr Martin Luther King, Jr. quoted in Douglas A. Hicks and Mark R. Valeri, *Global Neighbors: Christian Faith and Moral Obligation in Today's Economy*, Eerdmans Publishing, 2008.

a long way, a really long way – lifting us above even art, allowing us to glimpse – the art of living, the art of being immortal – and alive.'

Letter **B8** (632), to Bernard 23/6/1888

And although Vincent does not mention it by name, as he positioned Christ's parables at 'one of the highest summits reached by art' surely he was thinking not only of stories about prodigals, fig trees, sowers and harvests, but also of the one he chose to paint – the Good Samaritan.

Questions for discussion

Chapter 1: The Question ... 'And who is my neighbour?'

1. What do you think Jesus is saying to you today, in his Parable of the Good Samaritan?

2. How often have you thought about this parable before? Is it new to you or something with which you have grown up?

3. Why do you think Jesus taught in parables?
   Which are your favourites?
   Are there any you do not understand or perhaps with which you disagree?

4. At this early stage, to what extent do you identify with each of the four main players?
   The wounded man
   The Priest
   The Levite
   The Samaritan

5. How do you respond to van Gogh's doubts about God, or any higher power, intervening personally in our lives?

6. What do you make of van Gogh's version on the Good Samaritan?

7. Have you seen other paintings of this story? (There are some great ones out there, beyond van Gogh and Delacroix. Have a look on Google Images.)

Questions for discussion

8. What would a bullet-point guide to your spiritual life look like if you had to reduce it to only six paragraphs?

9. Where do your thoughts go when you think about eternity? What mental pictures or feelings does this concept bring to you? Are your thoughts 'lofty', with noble aspirations, angels, harps and clouds, or earthy, with salad grubs and gutters? Or are they something completely different?

Questions for discussion

Chapter 2: The Road from Jerusalem to Jericho

1. Can you imagine van Gogh's painting devoid of characters and showing just the bare landscape?
    a. How does it seem to you?
    b. Can you compare it with any places you have visited?
    c. Can you think of other notoriously dangerous locations?

2. What kind of terrain has your life's road crossed?
    a. Have you, thus far, enjoyed a reasonably straight run?
    b. Have you encountered twists, hairpin bends, rocks on the path or dead ends? (Feel free to call upon as many of your own metaphors as necessary.)

3. Is there a goal to your life?
    a. Would you want your life to be summed up in one line, such as '_____'s life's work was to ____', or 'They dedicated their life to _____'?
    b. How many people have the ability to control what their life is all about?
    c. If we have such goals, are these apparent from an early age, do they appear as we progress, or can they only be awarded with hindsight, possibly after our deaths?
    d. And if we do not know the true goals of our life, how do we know where to aim our efforts?

4. Do you agree with Vincent's analogy of the ship with two sails?
    a. Can we sail under the twin sails of both 'love' and the

'ambition'? And does this option truly occur to him?

b. Can you imagine sailing your ship without the sail called love? Where might it take you?

c. Do you think there are further sails that he does not acknowledge?

5. Do you have a vocation? Does God have a plan for your life?

a. How can we discover what this is?

b. Is anyone born with a vocation?

c. What will happen if you believe you have gone off-course?

d. What can we do to help others find and fulfil their vocations? Do we ever consider that our actions or attitudes might be stifling someone else's vocation?

e. How important is the way in which we pursue our vocation? Is caring for yourself an optional luxury, an absolute priority, or something in between?

f. How remarkable is your life in God's eyes? And how remarkable is the life of the person sitting next to you?

6. If at the end of your life you could conclude 'I have loved and I have been loved', would that be enough? Is there more you would wish to add?

Questions for discussion

Chapter 3: The Wounded Man and the Robbers

1. Do you ever see yourself or something of yourself in art? Is there a piece of music that perfectly captures your mood, or a painting that reveals your inner thoughts?

2. Have you encountered any wounded souls today? What were the outward signs of their struggles?

3. How prevalent, in your experience, is the pattern of sin, repentance and forgiveness, as a lens through which all else must be seen?
    a. Can this be useful?
    b. Have you ever found it damaging?
    c. Can you think of a time when fear or guilt have produced lasting fruit in your life?
    d. How often do you see Bible stories as 'sinful humans needing to repent'? Can you think of other ways of understanding God's grace to us?

4. How can those who have been badly wounded in love, ever love again?
    a. What would you say to van Gogh about his analogy, likening himself to a stony cliff, pounded by waves of desire?
    b. Could you truthfully console him that no one outgrows love?
    c. Would you advise him to find healing? And if so where would you send him?

Questions for discussion

5. What support can you offer to a person who might be at risk of self-harm or suicide?

Suicide Awareness

The story of Vincent van Gogh inevitably raises the subjects of self-harm and suicide. We have many more resources available to us today than existed in his time, to support people in crisis. The Zero Suicide Alliance (www.zerosuicidealliance.com) have an excellent free training package. It takes only twenty minutes to complete. One day, when you're not expecting it, it might prove to have been twenty minutes extremely well spent.

Questions for discussion

Chapter 4: The Priest

1. When you are facing difficult decisions ...
   a. How important are religious scriptures or doctrines?
   b. What is your way forward when different scriptural verses seem to contradict each other?
   c. Is there a hierarchy in your thinking, where certain verses take prominence over others?

2. How do you view the Priest?
   a. Do you sympathise with him at all?
   b. Do you judge him?
   c. Can you identify with him? Are you aware of ever 'passing by on the other side' and ignoring a fellow human in need?
   d. If the problem lies within the rules of his employer/religious institution, do you agree with the two duties laid out for him? (1. to protest against unloving rules, and 2. to stop anyway.)

3. Can you recall making any difficult decisions; those which placed you onto a good path and those which did not?
   a. Can you recall your thought processes?
   b. How often did you make your decision in the light of greater wisdom e.g. your scriptures or the advice of others?
   c. And have you ever made up your mind and only then sought scriptural wisdom to justify your decision?

4. If you belong to a church, does it welcome 'shaggy sheepdogs'?

5. What happens next for those too hurt by a religious institution to attend its services?

    a. What support do they need?

    b. What should the institution in question do for them?

    c. How does God see them?

    d. Where is God in the pain that surrounds such events?

    e. What support would you have offered to Vincent van Gogh as his trust in organised religion fell by the wayside? (As you ponder this, it would be wise to remember his quickness at spotting any 'Jesuitisms'.)

    f. Is there any wisdom you would like to offer to his father, Theodorus van Gogh? (Any allusions to Vincent's future, the auctions, the million-dollar price tags, the global fame, the museums, etc. come only from hindsight and therefore cannot be included in your answer.)

Questions for discussion

Chapter 5: The Levite

1. How important are your role models? If you had been the Levite, would you have allowed the Priest's decision to influence yours?

2. How inconvenient are your ethics?
   a. To yourself and your daily routines?
   b. To others?

3. Can you think of a time when someone who could have helped you passed by on the other side? Can you answer the flip-side of this question? How many people have you, like the Levite, recently passed by?

4. Should we fear a less than flattering role in someone else's story? If so, what steps might we take to minimise this happening?

5. Where in your life do you encounter your 'blank canvases'? What would it mean for you to follow van Gogh's advice and 'Just slap anything on when you see a blank canvas'?

6. How can we discover that which exists only in our blind spots?
   a. How often do we give ourselves time for reflection, away from the storms of passion?
   b. When did you last read something that completely changed your mind?

Questions for discussion

c. Can we help others to see better, without being that clumsy oaf who ignores the log in our own eye?[146]

7. How might the mantra 'recognise-the-human' affect your day?

---

[146] Matthew 7.1-5.

Questions for discussion

Chapter 6: The Samaritan

1. Vincent had strong views about religious art. Vibrant colours were better than haloes in his opinion.
   a. Do you agree?
   b. Which are your favourite religious works of art?
   c. Do you view any 'non-religious' pieces as religious?

2. Who have been the Good Samaritans in your life so far?
   a. Was this apparent at the time?
   b. Do you have a sense of being indebted to them? And, if so, how do you feel about this?
   c. How do feel about being in debt or under obligation to God?

3. How well do Theo and Jo van Gogh compare with Jesus' Samaritan?

4. What are your experiences of being 'moved with pity' or 'filled with compassion'?

5. Where and when do you feel safest? Which biblical images of safety appeal most to you?

6. How far can you identify with the wounded man's state of dire need?

7. What advice might you offer to Vincent, had he written to you with his analogy of the caged bird?

Questions for discussion

Chapter 7: 'Go and do likewise'

1. Can you think of times when you have tried to be a Good Samaritan, going out and doing likewise?
   a. How did you get on?
   b. Were you able to meet the needs of every neighbour or just a few?
   c. For how long were you able to keep this going?

2. Have you witnessed other people acting as Good Samaritans? What was their experience?

3. Can you imagine a conversation where someone approaches Jesus and asks, without trying to test him or trap him, 'How can I be good to my neighbour?'?
   a. How do you think Jesus might reply? (It might help to cobble together some of his other sayings.)
   b. Why do you think no one does ask this in the Gospels? (At least, there is no record of any such conversation.)

4. What questions would you ask Jesus about eternity? Would the lawyer's experience encourage you to phrase your question carefully, or simply avoid his type of question altogether?

5. How would you answer the question, 'How is God good to me?'? How easy would it be to do this without any references to, or echoes from the Parable of the Good Samaritan?

Appendix

The complete version of van Gogh's analogy of himself as a shaggy sheep dog.

I feel how Pa and Ma instinctively (I'm not saying reasonably) think about me.

There is a similar reluctance about taking me into their house as there would be about opening their home to a large shaggy dog. He will come into the living room with muddy paws – and also, he is just too shaggy. He will get in everyone's way and his bark is so loud.

Let's just say it, he's a dirty beast.

OK then – but this beast has a human history and although he's a dog, he has a human soul and a fine tuned one at that, and he can sense what people think about him, something an ordinary dog can't do.

And I, admitting that I'm kind of like a dog, all the same accept them for who they are.

So this home is too good for me, and Pa and Ma and the family present such a genteel facade (not underpinned by genuine feelings however) and – and there are clergy, many clergy. The dog understands that if he stays, it will be too much for them to endure, and his being 'in this house' would be barely tolerated, so he plans to find himself an actual dog-house elsewhere.

Now the dog is in fact Pa's son, and once too often Pa left him out on the street, where inevitably he became more unkempt, but since Pa forgot this fact years ago and he has never actually thought deeply enough about what the bond between father and son means, let's not talk about it any more.

But then – what if the dog bit someone? Or went mad? What if the local policeman had to come and shoot him dead?

Fine – yes to all that, most definitely, it'd be the right thing –

How about this then? Dogs can be guard dogs. But there's no call for that; as they say, it's peaceful and perfectly safe here, there's no trouble. So I'll shut up.

The dog has just one regret, which is that he didn't stay away; he wasn't as lonely out there on the heath as he is here in this house – despite the good intentions. This visit was a weakness on the part of the beast, which I hope will be forgotten by all concerned and which he'll avoid repeating ever again.

Letter **346** (413), to Theo 15/12/1883

I am that dog

OK my story was possibly slightly exaggerated – the reality is less pronounced, less extreme – but fundamentally I believe the rough caricature is truthful.

The shaggy sheepdog that I tried to sketch for you in yesterday's letter, is my character, and the beast's life is my life, though of course, I've omitted the details and only drafted out the essentials – possibly, it seems excessive to you – but I'm not taking anything back.

...

Let me tell you, *I'm making a conscious choice to follow the dog path*, I'm remaining a dog, I might be poor, l might be a painter, but at least I'm not giving up my human nature.

Letter **347** (414), to Theo 17/12/1883

Select bibliography

Memoir of Vincent van Gogh, Johanna van Gogh-Bonger, December, 1913 (which she wrote first in Dutch and then translated into English)

Poet & Peasant and Through Peasant Eyes, Kenneth E. Bailey, Eerdmanns, 1983

Short Stories by Jesus, The Enigmatic Parables of a Controversial Rabbi, Amy-Jill Levine, Harper-Collins, 2015

The Letters of Vincent van Gogh, selected and edited by Ronald de Leeuw, translated by Arnold Pomerans, Penguin Classics, 1997

Van Gogh and the Art of Living, The Gospel According to Vincent Van Gogh Anton Wessels, Wipf and Stock, 2013

Van Gogh's Ear, Bernadette Murphy, Vintage, 2017

Van Gogh: The Passionate Eye, Pascal Bonafoux, Thames and Hudson, 1987

Van Gogh, The Complete Paintings, Ingo F. Walther and Rainer Metzger, Taschen, 1989

Certain online resources have proved also invaluable:

www.biblegateway.com has been ever open on my desktop.

www.vggallery.com I am incredibly grateful to David

Brooks in Toronto. He is the creator of The Vincent van Gogh Gallery (www.vggallery.com) an incredible online catalogue of Van Gogh's works, paintings, drawing and letters.

www.vangoghletters.org The Van Gogh Museum keeps an online (and searchable) catalogue of his letters, in their original languages and also translated into English.

Acknowledgements

I am deeply indebted to many people who have supported me as I wrote this book:

My sincere thanks also go to the C. S. Lewis Company Ltd and to the Provost and Scholars of King's College, Cambridge and the Society of Authors as the E.M. Forster Estate for kindly permitting me to quote from (respectively) *The Four Loves* and *A Room With a View*.

My husband Haydn has been patient beyond any call of duty, especially on the many times I interrupted yet another conversation with a seemingly unconnected observation beginning, 'Well in van Gogh's letters ...', 'Van Gogh on the other hand ...' and on, and on. The first version of this book was written during a lockdown in which we had no access to a working printer. Haydn therefore sat and listened as I read each finished chapter from the screen. His comments were invaluable.

Eddie Thomas went through the script with a fine toothcomb, correcting my wayward grammar, my inconsistent punctuation and offering invaluable reflections about the overall flow and tone of the book. Charl DeWinter spent several Zoom sessions patiently correcting my translations of van Gogh's Dutch, bringing that level of insight possessed only by a native speaker. Jennie Day and Tony Thwaites listened supportively to my earliest babbling enthusiasms and never complained about the many van Gogh books that appeared in random places around their home. Tony took a great deal of time to read through some of my first ideas and, like the expert gardener, pruned a couple of unfruitful branches, while encouraging the good shoots. Ian Wallis revived a former role and once again helped me with some questions about the New Testament. David Moloney and all the team at DLT have supported and encouraged me at every stage. I am also very grateful to two people whom I will never meet: Henri Nouwen and Sister Wendy Beckett. Their writings opened to me the inexpressible value of praying while meditating on art.

Throughout my time researching and writing I have thought constantly of my own father, Trevor Martin. This book is dedicated to his memory. There is a lot in van Gogh's letters about complicated relationships between fathers and sons. And there is also love, deep love, if not always agreement. My father and I did not see eye to eye on everything but we shared so many good things, including a love of art. I think out of anything I will ever write, this book is the one that would have appealed the most to him, because despite many differences, we shared together a deep appreciation for the work of Vincent van Gogh.